$100M Money Models

How To Make Money

Summary & Workbook

ALEX HORMOZI

Disclaimer

The information provided in this book is for educational and informational purposes only. The author, publisher, and licensed distributor have made reasonable efforts to ensure that the information within was accurate at the time of publication. The author, publisher, and licensed distributor make no representation or warranties with respect to the merchantability, fitness for a particular purpose, current or continued accuracy or completeness, and reliability of the contents of this book.

The strategies, tips, and tools discussed in this book are the author's personal opinions and are provided as-is. They are intended to provide helpful and informative material on the subjects addressed in this book. Success in any marketing and business endeavors is based on a wide range of factors unique to each individual or business.

Laws are subject to change and may vary by location and jurisdiction. You, as the reader, are encouraged to consult with a professional where appropriate and review the current local laws before implementing any marketing strategies or campaigns.

Earnings and income representations made by the author are aspirational statements only of your potential earnings. The success of the author and others referenced herein, testimonials, and other examples used are exceptional, non-typical results and are not intended to be and are not a guarantee that you or others will achieve the same results. Individual results will always vary and your results will depend entirely on your individual capacity, work ethic, business, skills and experience, level of motivation, diligence in applying the strategies discussed, the economy, the normal and unforeseen risks of doing business, and other factors within or beyond your control.

No guarantee is made that you will achieve any result at all from the ideas in this book. The author, publisher, and licensed distributor disclaim any representations or warranties (express or implied), including, without limitation, those of merchantability, fitness for any particular purpose, current or continued accuracy or completeness, and reliability. Reliance on the information provided is solely at your own risk. As further described herein, the author, publisher, and licensed distributor shall in no event be held liable to you or any party for any direct, indirect, punitive, special, incidental, speculative, or other consequential damages arising directly or indirectly from any use and/or misuse of this book, which is provided "as is", and without warranties.

As always, the advice of a competent legal, tax, accounting, finance, or other professional should be sought and obtained.

Any statements that express or involve discussions with respect to predictions, goals, expectations, beliefs, plans, projections, objectives, assumptions or future events or performance are not statements of historical fact and may be "forward looking statements." Forward looking statements are based on expectations, estimates, and projections at the time the statements are made that involve a number of risks and uncertainties which could cause actual results or events to differ materially from those presently anticipated.

Running a business involves the risk of loss as well as the possibility of profit. All businesses involve risk, and all business decisions remain the responsibility of the individual. The author, Bumble IP, LLC, Acquisition.com, LLC, and their affiliates (collectively referred to herein as the "Company") have not made any guarantees that the strategies outlined in this book will be profitable or beneficial for you or your business, and the Company is not liable for any potential business losses related to these strategies.

The Company's representatives are professionals, and their results are not typical of the average individual. Background, education, effort, and dedication of individuals and business owners will affect their overall experience. Any examples shared in this book are merely illustrative and not guarantees of a return on businesses or other result. Each reader's results may vary. The Company does not warrant the performance, effectiveness, or applicability of any sites listed or linked in this book. All links are for informational purposes only and are not warranted for content, accuracy, or any other implied or explicit purpose. All the information provided in this book pertaining to running a business and business strategies is educational only and not specific guarantees of success. Even though reasonable precaution has been taken in the preparation of this book, the Company does not assume any liability for errors and/or omissions. This book is published without warranty or guarantee of any kind, either expressed or implied. The Company is not liable for any damages, regardless of whether arising directly or indirectly from the use and/or misuse of this book. Readers agree to release and hold harmless the Company and its members, employees, agents, representatives, affiliates, subsidiaries, successors, and assignees (collectively "Agents") from and against any and all claims, liabilities, losses, causes of actions, costs, lost profits, lost opportunities, indirect, special, incidental, consequential, punitive, or any other damages whatsoever and expenses (including, without limitation, court costs and attorney's fees) ("Losses") asserted against, resulting from, imposed upon or incurred by any of the Agents as a result of, or arising out of the reader's use and/or misuse of this book. This book is intended for informational and educational purposes only.

HYPOTHETICAL PERFORMANCE RESULTS HAVE MANY INHERENT LIMITATIONS, SOME OF WHICH ARE DESCRIBED BELOW. NO REPRESENTATION IS BEING MADE THAT ANY BUSINESS WILL OR IS LIKELY TO ACHIEVE PROFITS OR LOSSES SIMILAR TO THOSE SHOWN OR DESCRIBED. IN FACT, THERE ARE FREQUENTLY SHARP DIFFERENCES BETWEEN HYPOTHETICAL PERFORMANCE RESULTS AND THE ACTUAL RESULTS SUBSEQUENTLY ACHIEVED BY ANY PARTICULAR BUSINESS. ONE OF THE LIMITATIONS OF HYPOTHETICAL PERFORMANCE RESULTS IS THAT THEY ARE GENERALLY PREPARED WITH THE BENEFIT OF HINDSIGHT. IN ADDITION, HYPOTHETICAL BUSINESS DOES NOT INVOLVE FINANCIAL RISK, AND NO HYPOTHETICAL BUSINESS RECORD CAN COMPLETELY ACCOUNT FOR THE IMPACT OF FINANCIAL AND OTHER RISK IN ACTUAL BUSINESS. FOR EXAMPLE, THE ABILITY TO WITHSTAND LOSSES OR TO ADHERE TO A PARTICULAR BUSINESS STRATEGY IN SPITE OF BUSINESS LOSSES ARE MATERIAL POINTS WHICH CAN ALSO ADVERSELY AFFECT ACTUAL BUSINESS RESULTS. THERE ARE NUMEROUS OTHER FACTORS RELATED TO THE MARKETS IN GENERAL OR TO THE IMPLEMENTATION OF ANY SPECIFIC BUSINESS PROGRAM, WHICH CANNOT BE FULLY ACCOUNTED FOR IN THE PREPARATION OF HYPOTHETICAL PERFORMANCE. When used herein, this "book" means this book, its contents, and all information and ideas contained therein.

Copyright © 2025 by Bumble IP, LLC and distributed via license by Acquisition.com, LLC. Reproduction or translation of any part of this work beyond that permitted by Section 107 or 108 of the 1976 United States Copyright Act without the permission of the copyright owner is unlawful. Acquisition.com®, its logo, and $100M® are all registered trademarks of Bumble IP, LLC and utilized via limited license by Acquisition.com, LLC. All rights reserved, including rights for text and data mining and training of artificial technologies or similar technologies.

Contents

How to Use This Workbook & Summary 1

Start Here 3

Section I: What's A Money Model? 7
The Four Types of Offers That Make Money Models 11

Section II: Attraction Offers 13
Win Your Money Back 15
Giveaways 20
Decoy Offer 25
Buy X Get Y Free 30
Pay Less Now or Pay More Later 36
Free Goodwill Offer 41
Attraction Conclusion 43

Section III: Upsell Offers 45
The Classic Upsell 48
Menu Upsells 53
Anchor Upsell 58
Rollover Upsell 62
Upsell Offers Conclusion 66

Section IV: Downsell Offers 67
Payment Plan Downsells 69
Trial With Penalty 73
Feature Downsells 79
Downsell Offers Conclusion 84

Section V: Continuity Offers 85
Continuity Bonus Offers 87
Continuity Discount Offers 92
Waived Fee Offer 98
Continuity Offers Conclusion 102

Section VI: Make Your Money Model 103
Ten Years In Ten Minutes 109
Final Thoughts 113
Free Goodies 115

HOW TO USE THIS WORKBOOK & SUMMARY

Many people buy summaries and workbooks because authors do a poor job editing their fluff. With *$100M Money Models*, this is not the case. The entire book is only ~187 pages with big font and lots of pictures and 3.5 hours spoken slowly as an audiobook. Most people can read it in one sitting. It's short already. So in this summary, I did three things different from the book:

1) I summarized the stories

2) I removed the majority of examples. If you don't understand a concept, check out the videos that come for free with this book on my site at **acquisition.com/training**

3) I swapped the chapter recaps for workbook exercises

The result of these changes is a workbook that cuts the word count of the original book roughly in half. That being said, if you read faster than you listen (most people), you can read the entire bestselling book in about 3.5 hours. This one should take you about half the time (60–120 minutes depending on your reading speed).

If you've already read the book, use this as a review and focus on the exercises.

If you haven't read the main book, you will get what you need to apply the main concepts in your business.

START HERE

Where I slept at my first gym: my "concrete bedroom."

So, I'm flat broke and living in my gym. I'd gone against everyone's advice. And when my gym wasn't printing money, I got scared. Fast.

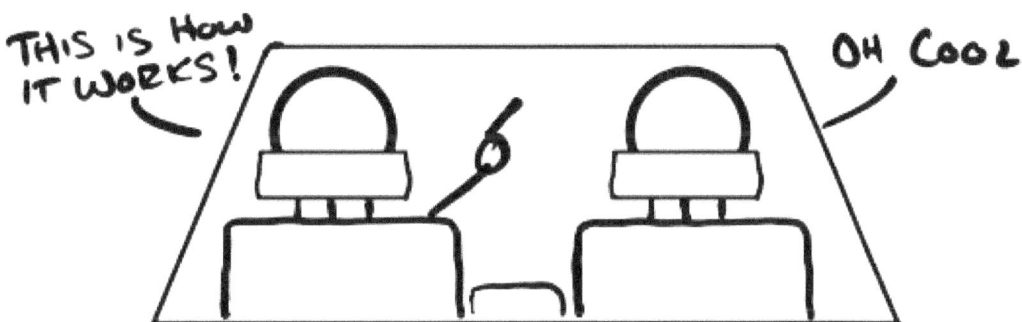

This guy who owned some storage units across the street joins my gym. He notices I'm struggling and takes me out for breakfast. That's when he schools me on how to really make money in business. He drives me to his facility and walks me through all these tiny little details he used to make money. It was mind-blowing stuff, like how a "free" month of storage actually makes them $127. This was the first time I got exposed to multi-step sales processes and multiple offers layered together in a row to maximize profit. Years later, I'd refer to these as "Money Models."

***

Fast forward a couple of years, and I've got six gyms running. I'm feeling pretty good about myself, so I pay this big-shot marketer for advice. I tell him how I open gyms—you know, pre-selling memberships, using that money for equipment and all.

Here's the kicker: When I tell him I'm spending $5 per lead and making $680 per customer, he's floored. It turns out that what I thought was just okay was actually amazing.

But then he hits me with this: "You shouldn't be running gyms." I'm thinking, "What the heck?" But then he explains I've got a great skill set in a crappy business. He says I should be teaching other gym owners my methods instead.

It was hard to swallow, but the guy was making way more than me. So, I figured I'd better listen. And that's how I ended up completely changing my business.

***

After that conversation, I closed my newest gym and sold the other five over the next ninety days. It was wild. But it freed me up to go all in on this new thing: Gym Launch.

For the next couple of years, I flew all over the place, turning gyms around. I did 30 or so gym turnarounds. Then I thought, "Why am I killing myself traveling?" So I switched to a licensing model. Basically, I'd help gym owners follow our proven system to fill their gyms and make money, all without me having to show up in person.

Now, it was a pretty niche market, but man, these gym owners were in pain. Some were literally struggling to eat. But once they filled their gym in a month, word spread like wildfire. Gym Launch exploded.

Over the next five years, I took home over $43 million in distributions. Then, I sold 66% of the company for $46.2 million, all cash. Crazy, right? I hit $100 million net worth at 31. Trust me, no one was more shocked than I was.

After that, my wife and I started this family office thing called Acquisition.com. We invest in businesses we know how to grow. Our portfolio now? It's doing over $200 million a year. We've got our fingers in everything—brick and mortar chains, software, services, e-commerce, you name it.

The funny thing is, even though we're in all these different industries, we're still using the same principles I used back in my gym days. It's all in this summary of *$100M Money Models*.

And here's a picture in front of our headquarters now in 2025. Fancy right?

So What's In It For You?

In about a page, I took you from struggling to making ends meet to crossing $100,000,000 in net worth. So the natural question is… how? Answer: *by making more money from customers than it costs to get them.* And that's what this book, *$100M Money Models*, is all about.

Since I've been in business, the landscape has changed more than once. And it'll keep changing. The good news is that sound principles help you print money no matter what. I've learned a lot of Money Models. I cover my favorites here.

$100M Money Models shows <u>already proven</u> offers you can use <u>today</u>. And, the instructions to make them happen. Think of *$100M Money Models* as a book of winning lottery tickets—all you have to do is cash them in.

Also, I want to make something clear, *these are my private notes.* If it's here, I've made money with it. These chapters contain my observations and experiences with different businesses. From local chains, to physical products, to services, education, software, and so on. And they were scattered everywhere over the years. *Until now.*

<u>This is my cookbook for making money.</u>

How This Book Is Structured

This book teaches you *one* insanely profitable thing: **how to build a $100M Money Model**. With a $100M Money Model, *you make so much money in the first 30 days that the cost of getting more customers will never be a problem again.* With so many customers, you'll be forced to work on *everything else* in your business to just keep up! A problem for another book to solve (winky face).

Book Outline

Start Here & Problem This Book Solves: *You just finished it*

Section I: What's a Money Model? *Coming up next...*

Section II: Attraction Offers

Section III: Upsell Offers

Section IV: Downsell Offers

Section V: Continuity Offers

Section VI: Make Your Money Model

That's it. Easy peasy. Let's get to it.

SECTION I:
WHAT'S A MONEY MODEL?

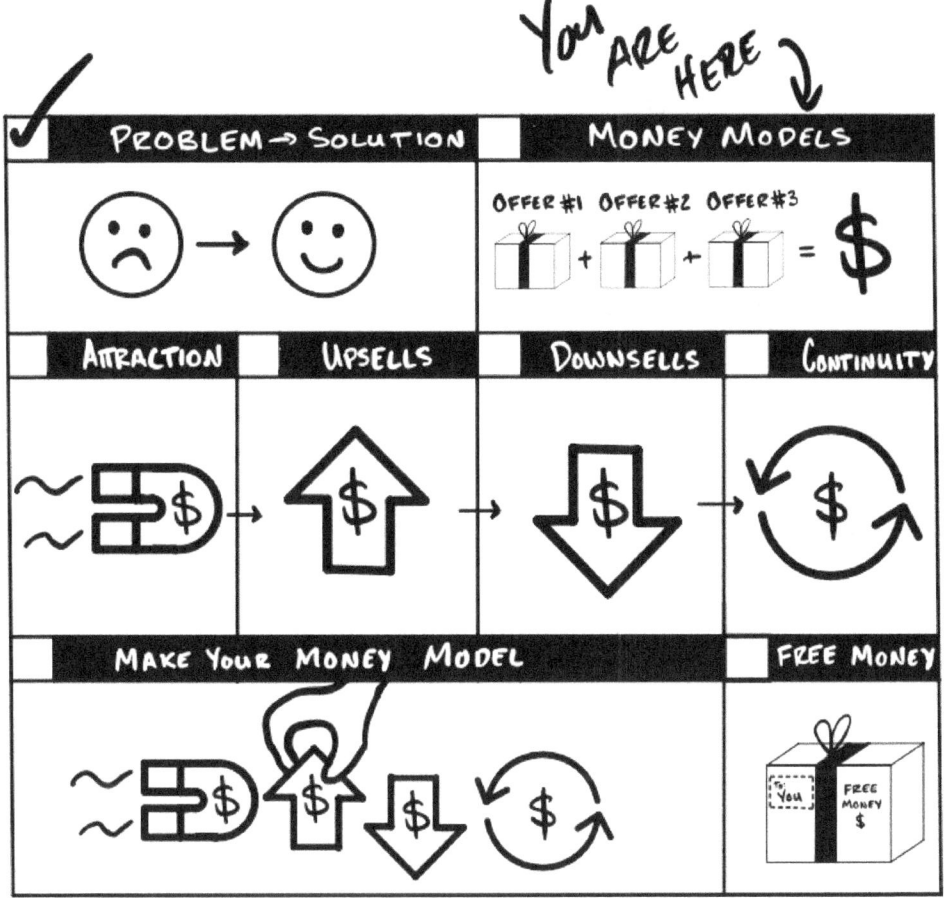

Rental Car Story

So, I'm at this car rental place, right? I go in for a cheap $19 a day car, but watch this. The agent starts offering me all these upgrades—a roomier truck, late return, better insurance, prepaid fuel. I'm like, "Yeah, sure," to most of it, not paying attention.

Then, as I'm walking to my car, I see the receipt and BAM! I realize I'm paying $100 a day instead of $19. Five times what I planned!

But here's the thing—they knew exactly what I'd want before I did. They solved problems I didn't even know I'd have. That's a killer Money Model right there. And if they didn't have a model that was profitable, they probably wouldn't be in business. And I wouldn't have a car.

A Money Model Happened

A Money Model is a *sequence of offers*. At their core, we find every opportunity to solve a customer's problem… and then offer to solve it. For that reason, Money Models tend to have many offers in a specific order. If you offer the right thing when customers realize they need it, you can make *as many offers as you like*.

This is the rental car company's Money Model stated plainly:

<u>Offer #1</u> Vehicle Upgrade

<u>Offer #2</u> Late Return

<u>Offer #3</u> Premium Insurance

<u>Offer #4</u> Minimum Insurance Downsell

<u>Offer #5</u> Prepaid Gas

So yeah, I paid more, *but it also solved more problems.* Let's break down the problems the rental car agent solved for me:

- She solved my "big man in a small car" problem by *offering* a vehicle that had more space.

- She solved my "late checkout" problem by *offering* the flexibility to keep the vehicle longer.

- She solved my "worries about dinging the car" by *offering* insurance to protect against it.

- She solved my "risk of missing my flight" problem by *offering* a way to prepay for the gas ahead of time so I wouldn't have to do it on my ride back.

    …And all those things cost money *I was happy to pay.*

The rental car company thought out every nuance. They told me about the problem, then *made their solution available to me.* They offer solutions for higher fees and hassles I might have had later for smaller fees in total *right now.*

As a result, my $19 rental became a $100 rental. I paid *more money faster.* And now, we can see why the car rental industry brings in billions in the United States alone… *per month.* A successful Money Model.

Beware: Bad Money Models Kill Businesses

Many businesses lose money getting customers, leading to a vicious cycle:

- Spend on advertising
- Realize losses
- Cut back on marketing
- Get fewer customers
- Resort to personal funds or loans
- Struggle for months or years to break even
- Potentially lose everything

This doesn't have to happen. There's money to be made, but you need to know how to get it. Traditional businesses rely on profit building up over time to cover the costs of getting customers. This works for big companies or those with investors, but it's risky for small, bootstrapped businesses. (Probably you).

Example: Spending $100 to acquire a customer who brings $500 profit sounds great. But if it takes two years to recoup that money, you might run out of cash first.

You have two choices:

1) Wait years to get paid and hope you survive
2) Get paid fast and grow as much as you want

A good Money Model is option 2.

Good Money Models Make Millionaires

If you make more offers, and people buy them, you make more money. If you make more money, you can use it to get more customers. If they pay you that money faster, you can get those customers faster *and* stay profitable.

But what if you make your customers twice as valuable, you get twice as many of them, and get those customers at twice the speed?… *your business grows 8x faster*. And if you triple them… *your business grows 27x faster*. See where I'm going with this? You can get really big, really profitable, really fast… *with just a few changes*. And that's exactly what I'm gonna show you how to do.

Next Up

Money Models are a sequence of offers. Different offers solve different problems. So if you want to win, you have to figure out what to offer *next*. To figure that out, you've gotta understand *The Four Offer Types*…

The Four Types of Offers That Make Money Models

Making one offer works better than making none. And making more offers works better than making one. Combining offers in a sequence makes a Money Model. My Money Models combine four different offer types.

Four Types of Offers

There are four types of offers: Attraction Offers, Upsell Offers, Downsell Offers, and Continuity Offers. All improve our Money Model, but they all do it *differently*. They work great on their own, but together they make your business unstoppable.

1) **Attraction Offers** turn strangers into customers.

2) **Upsell Offers** get people to spend more cash.

3) **Downsell Offers** get people to say yes when they would have said no.

4) **Continuity Offers** keep people buying.

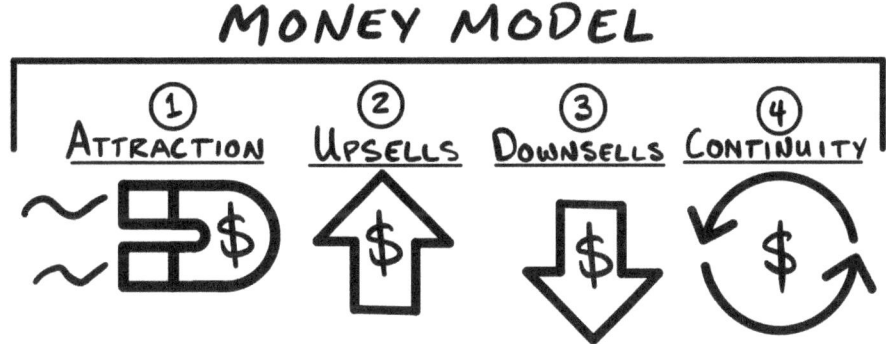

If you look at great businesses, you'll see different versions of these offers as core components of their money-making engine. You can use one, two, multiples of one, or all four together. You can combine them however you want. But, when I look at *my* most profitable businesses, I used all four. So that's what I recommend.

How I Structured The Sections

I start with Attraction Offers, because if you're not getting customers, you need one of those first. Then, we cover Upsell Offers, followed by Downsell Offers. Then to finish the four types, I show you my favorite Continuity Offers *exactly how I learned them*.

How Each Chapter is Structured

Here's how the rest of the book reads:

1) **Doodle** directly from my notes. Exactly as I drew it. It helped me remember it, so it will help you remember it, too.

2) **Story** (summary) of how I first learned this Money Model.

3) **Description** of how the Money Model works.

4) **Examples** of them being used by real businesses in the real world.

5) **Important Notes** and tactics that make the Money Model work. These tidbits help you execute the play—like it's your hundredth time doing it—*on your first try*.

6) **Exercise** to apply the chapter to your business.

7) **Accompanying free video training course** that comes with each offer in this book you can find at: acquisition.com/training/money

Important Notes Before Getting Started

1) **If a customer asks for their money back—*Give it back*.**

2) **Instead of saying, "This won't work," ask, "How can I make this work?"**

3) **Avoid hard selling.** Offer solutions when customers have problems. If they're not interested, move on.

4) **Obey the law.** Advertising regulations change often, so consult lawyers about offer legality.

5) **State the facts and tell the truth.** If your facts aren't compelling, change reality until they become compelling. Don't lie.

Any Offer Can Be Used On Its Own, At Any Time, in Any Order. A business works as long as it makes a profit. Most offers in this book could meet that minimum requirement *on their own*. When used in the right sequence, and at the right time, they make a *$100M Money Model*.

SECTION II: ATTRACTION OFFERS

How to turn eyeballs into money

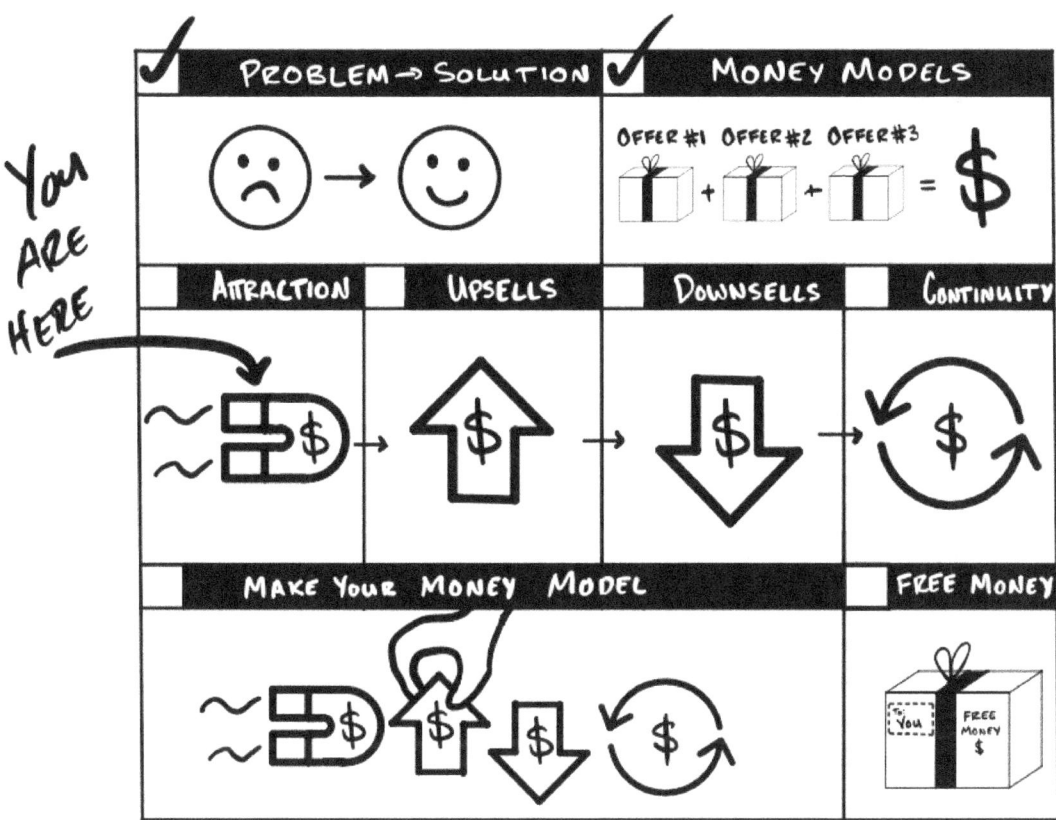

Attraction offers generate leads *and* convert them into customers. They turn advertising into money by offering something free or at a discount. We do this because everyone wants a great deal. In a great deal, customers get *far* more value than the price they pay. Strangers can only take your word on the value. But, they absolutely understand the price. For that reason, discounts make *anything* a great deal to just about *anyone*. And, the greater the discount, the better the deal. The greatest discount of all being *free*.

First off, any time I say "free," you can also use "discount" or "$1." Any time I use "discount," you can also use "free" or "$1" and so on. They all discount a product to some level—even if you discount it by 100%! If you can imagine a way to use a discount or a free offer… then you can do it. After that, I'll let you use your noggin to swap them as you see fit.

So How Do You Make Money By Offering Free Stuff?

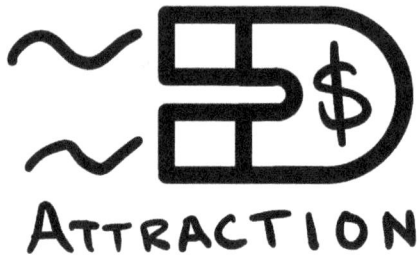

Think about it this way—people look for one thing and then buy another by accident *all the time*. Attraction Offers get them to do it *on purpose*. But what's a better deal than free stuff? *More and better free stuff.* One free thing is awesome. Two free things are awesomer. And, maybe to get those two free things, *they have to buy one*. That's how we make money on free stuff.

In this section, I go over my five favorite ways to make money by offering free stuff:

1) Win Your Money Back

2) Giveaways

3) Decoy Offer

4) Buy X Get Y Free

5) Pay Less Now or Pay More Later

Let's make some money.

Win Your Money Back

If you do x or achieve y within z days, you can get it free.

Story: June 2013

A gym owner, Danny, shared a new offer that was crushing it for him. Here's how he stumbled on it.

A difficult client proposed a deal: $500 for eight weeks of training, refundable if he hit his goal, in exchange for using his before and after pictures for marketing. The client lost the weight, got his money back, then bought more training. And, advertising his before and after pictures got Danny a bunch of referrals. Danny made so much money from it that he started offering the deal to everyone. And the "win your money back" offer was born. He taught it to me and I've used it ever since.

Description

A Win Your Money Back Offer works like this. *You* set a goal for the customer *and* tell them how to reach it. If they reach it, then they qualify to get their money back *or* get it back as store credit.

To "Win Your Money Back," the person has three options: Get Results, Take Actions, or both. And to make this work, you have to make the results and actions *simple* to track.

Results: Here, no matter what they do, if the customer gets the result, they win their money back. For example: Making $X a month, Getting Y customers, Losing Z lbs, etc. *Basically, they bet on their own ability to reach the goal.*

Actions: Here, you hold them accountable for *doing* actions instead of *getting* results. No matter what results they get, if the customer does what you ask, they win their money back. For example: attend all sessions, calls, meetings, log progress, take pictures, do assigned homework, etc. *Here, they bet on their ability to follow directions.*

Actions *and* Results: Here, you hold customers accountable for following directions and getting results. If they do both, they win their money back. Often, people wanting to achieve a goal have too few skills to do it. Even if they did bet on themselves, they'd fail. By setting a good goal for them *and* showing how they reach it, they have a fighting chance. *Here they bet on their ability to follow directions and that your directions will get them the result.*

Bottom line: Customers put money down. If they do the stuff OR they get the result OR both—*they get it back as cash or store credit.*

Examples

Business To Consumer Offer: Free 28-Day Blueprint

Deposit X dollars and get it all back if you:

- ☐ Attend all your consulting calls.
- ☐ Post your progress in the group once per week.
- ☐ Journal daily in our app.
- ☐ Attend your feedback session and your transformation session.

(Hint: calls and meetings become opportunities to make more offers.)

Business To Business Offer: 5 Customers In 5 Days Free Challenge

Deposit X dollars and get it all back if you:

- ☐ Send 100 messages per day.
- ☐ Report stats on messages sent.
- ☐ Attend daily training.

- ☐ Post finished homework in the group.
- ☐ Attend the day 5 consulting call.

    (Hint: here you offer more, better, or new products and services.)

Physical Product Offer: Put 1,000,000 Miles On Your Car, And Get A Free Car

Get a free car if you:

- ☐ Buy a new car from us.
- ☐ Drive the car 1,000,000 miles.
- ☐ Turn it in.
- ☐ Take pictures and be in a press release.
- ☐ We'll credit all your original purchase price towards your next car.

    (This was an actual offer.)

Important Points

Win Your Money Back is magical for businesses that require their customers to put in continuous efforts to get their ideal outcome.

- The Win Your Money Back Offer rocks because:
    - o You get loads of up front cash.
    - o You get more customers to say yes since you lower their risk.
    - o You get massive results for customers.
    - o You get more long-term customers.
    - o They advertise your offer to get you even more customers.
- Making some meetings a part of getting the deposit back gives great opportunities to check-in with your customers and make more offers specific to their needs.
- Everyone thinks businesses make money on people who fail the program. No. The real money comes from people who succeed with it *and you have something else to offer them*. Trust me on this one. The more results you deliver, the more money you'll make. Think long.

- Make refund criteria easy to track, aligned with customer goals, and helpful for the business.

- Only use a Win Your Money Back Offer if your refund rate is below 5%. Otherwise, fix your product before doing this. You risk getting too many refunds.

- Put the store credit toward another, preferably more expensive, offer. You want them to stay customers… so give them the opportunity. You never want people to stop paying you.

- To make more sales and keep more customers, make everyone a winner in private. That way, everyone stays surprised and grateful when you make your Upsell Offer.

Exercise #1: Create Your Win Your Money Back Offer

1. Write down what the customer has to do or achieve (or both) to qualify to win their money back. Remember, make them *easy to track*.

    a. Actions they must take to qualify for their money back:

        i. Advertising for you _____

        ii. Sales meetings they must attend _____

        iii. Actions they take to succeed _____

    _____

    _____

    b. Result: _____

2. Decide whether you want them to win back money or store credit:

    a. Money ( )

    b. Credit ( )

3. Figure out a more expensive follow-up offer (that costs 5x your original offer) to apply the credit to: _____

FREE GIFT: Win Your Money Back Offers Video Training

I've made a tremendous amount of money with this offer and I have more details and stories I couldn't reasonably fit in the book. If you want that, I made a free video for you, no opt-in required. To watch it, just go to acquisition.com/training/money. You can also scan the QR code if you hate typing.

Giveaways

One lucky winner gets a free year… enter here!

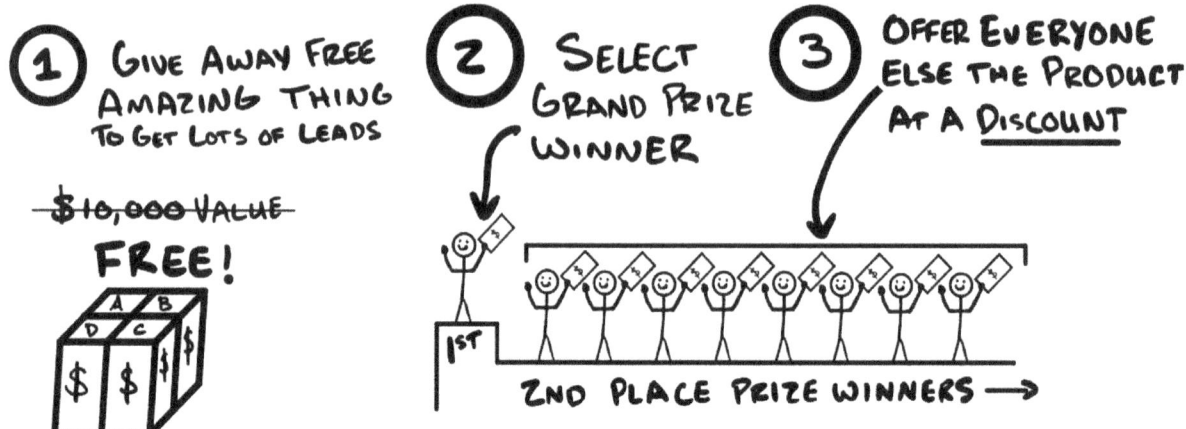

Story

So, I was chatting with this guy who runs a fitness certification business. He told me about this crazy smart way they get leads. Check this out:

They advertise a full-ride scholarship for their program. People apply and share why they should get picked. Then, one person wins the full ride. But here's the kicker—they give partial scholarships to pretty much everyone else.

When they call these people to tell them about their partial scholarship, they're super excited. Most sign up right there on the spot. The genius part? These folks don't know the actual price up front, but they know the value of the full scholarship. So when they hear the discounted price, it feels like a steal.

It works so well they sometimes have to limit sign-ups. And get this—they teach this same money model to the trainers they certify. Meaning, it works for business-to-business offers just as well as business-to-consumer offers. At the end of the day, Free Giveaways generate many leads who show interest in *your most expensive product*. What could be better?

Description

Giveaway Offers advertise a chance to win a big prize in exchange for contact information and whatever else you want. Then, after picking a winner, you offer everyone else the big prize at a discounted price. Giveaways also go by names like "sweepstakes" and "raffles" etc. They all mean "enter for a chance to win." To run a Giveaway Offer you:

1) Pick A Grand Prize. Make your Grand Prize *the thing you want everyone to buy*. Make sure you assign a monetary value to your grand prize to serve as a price anchor for your second-place prize. For instance, if you sell $5,000 worth of value for $2,000, then advertise the $5,000 value! If you want more referrals, give two grand prizes away. Tell them if someone they refer wins, they win the other grand prize.

2) Pick Your Participation Trophy/Partial Scholarship Prize. The partial scholarship prize is a *discount* on the Grand Prize. And the bigger the discount, the more compelling the offer. (Hint: so the bigger the value you assign your Grand Prize, the better!) Remember, leads entered the Giveaway because they found the Grand Prize interesting. The partial scholarship prize gets you customers because you offer what they *already showed interest in* at a discount.

The "discount" was the "partial scholarship" in the story. Call your partial scholarship whatever you want for your business: scholarship, gift card, dollars off, store credit, vouchers, etc.

3) Ask For Contact Information in exchange for a chance to win. Beyond that, I survey for prize *eligibility* and then ask them to take *qualifying actions*.

4) Eligibility: I ask if they're a fit for my products. Like *"Do you own a vet clinic?"* or more character/need-based questions like *"Why should you be selected?"* You can get great information from every lead because you can make it part of the entry process. Get information that indicates how your offer will provide them value. This becomes important for making offers later.

5) Qualifying Actions: other stuff entrants do to qualify to win. I also use these to get them to promote my giveaway more, or demonstrate higher levels of interest. Ex: attending a call or event, making a post, entering a group, etc.

6) Put The Giveaway On A Deadline To Add Urgency. Make your Giveaway more urgent by only making it available for a limited time. I like three to seven days. As soon as leads enter the Giveaway—update them daily. First, let them know how long they have left until you announce the winner. You can do this with email, direct messages, texts, social media posts, and so on. Do as many as reasonable. Once a day across all platforms works fine. Second, provide value along with your countdown. Show everyone the benefits of the grand prize, how excited they should be, and *refer everyone to social proof*. Keep the hype alive! Run your Giveaway for seven days, or until the entries hit however many people you can manage to call in seven days—whichever comes first.

7) Announce The Grand Prize Winner And Start Contacting Everyone Else. Announce the Grand Prize winner publicly, then message everyone else who qualifies privately. That's the magic—*as many people can win the partial scholarship/discount as you want*. Notify them by text, email, and direct messages. In that message, ask them to schedule a call to redeem their prize.

To make sure they redeem their partial prize, add another deadline. Make claiming the partial scholarship prize expire in seven days. The second countdown works like the first: show the benefits, more social proof, and more valuable stuff about your offer. Give them a way to book a call to claim their prize. If you have problems with people missing appointments, and the law allows it, charge no-show fees. This will get more people to show up.

Explain to the partial scholarship winners the cost-to-value *using their discount*. My rule of thumb: make your partial scholarship discount equal to 10–30% of your Gross Margins. Say we advertise a Grand Prize with a "$5,000 value" with a $2,000 retail price tag. The partial scholarship winner gets it for $1,800 (a 10% discount off retail). When we let them know they won the partial scholarship, we explain they get $5,000 in value for an $1,800 price tag. By comparing the value of the thing to what they pay, a 10% discount becomes a 64% difference in cost-to-value!

If somebody says "no" to your main discount offer, have another product or service to discount. It may suit the lead better.

Bottom Line: Remember, everyone that entered the Giveaway showed interest in your thing. And if somebody shows interest in a thing you have to offer—*offer it to them*.

Example Free Giveaways

Dentist Offer—Free Perfect Smile Giveaway

Grand Prize: A free set of invisible braces—$6,000 retail price

Partial Scholarship/Promotional Offer: $2,000 gift card for braces

Physical Products Offer—Free Year of Organic Dog Food

Grand Prize: Free Year of Organic Dog Food—$1,000 retail price

Partial Scholarship/Promotional Offer: $300 gift card for dog food *only useable with a one-year subscription*

Services Offer—Free Ultimate Giveaway

Grand Prize: Free 1-Year Package—$5,000 retail price

Partial Scholarship/Promotional Offer: $2,000 voucher redeemable toward 1-Year Service Agreement

Consulting Offer—Free 16-Week Turnaround Giveaway

Grand Prize: 16-Week Turnaround—$12,000 retail price

Partial Scholarship/Promotional Offer: $6,000 Partial Scholarship

Exercise #2: Create Your Giveaway Offer

1. Pick Your Grand Prize: _____
    a. Pick whether you want to double the prize to incentivize referrals (Y / N)
2. Pick Your Partial Scholarship Offer: _____
3. Write Out the Information You Want to Collect:
    a. Contact Information: _____
    b. Eligibility Criteria: _____
    c. Actions They Must Take: _____
4. Set Deadline for: _____
    a. End of Drawing Deadline: _____
    b. End of Ability to Claim Prize: _____

FREE GIFT: Giveaways Bonus Training

Giveaways are one of the strongest attraction offers on earth. They're so good they need to be regulated. I mean—who doesn't want somethin' for nothin', right? I made a free video training that covers the topic in depth. If you love this stuff as much as me, you can check it out at acquisition.com/training/money. As always, you can also scan the QR code if you hate typing. Enjoy.

Decoy Offer

Which one do you think will get you the best results?

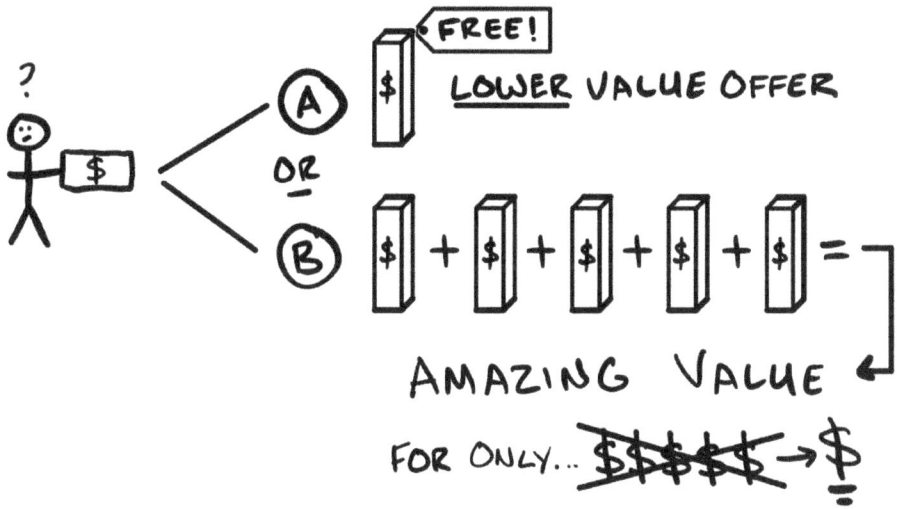

Story

John was my second mentor. He was this retired businessman who'd invite me out to his lake house. We'd ride in his truck and he'd tell me stories for hours. He'd drop all these business nuggets on me—stuff about price vs. value, low-cost offers, you name it.

One day, he tells me about this genius thing they did at his tanning salon—the 5-Day $5 VIP Tanning Pass. Here's why it worked: everyone thinks they can get tan in five days. But they can't, not really. So when people come in, they give them this whole spiel about not burning, like cooking a turkey too fast. Then they'd say, "Hey, why not just apply this $5 pass to a monthly membership? It's only $19.99 for unlimited tanning. And way cheaper than paying $25 per tanning session." People saw the value. Easy upsell.

Fast forward five years, and I'm running my gym business. We hit a snag—our fitness leads got crazy expensive. I'm wracking my brain for a solution, and then I remember John's tanning pass method.

So we tried something similar. We offered a cheap option to get people in the door, but then hit 'em with this premium "Ultimate" package for $399. It had all the bells and whistles, plus a guarantee. And the best part—70–80% of people went for the pricier option. We were killing it again.

The big takeaway? Give customers what they want now, so you can give them what they need later. And always make your premium offer the clear winner. That's the art of the Decoy Offer. John taught me the secret: you gotta know what your customers need better than they do.

Description

Decoy Offers advertise something free or discounted. Then, when leads ask to learn more, you *also* present a more valuable premium offer. The premium offer provides more features, benefits, bonuses, guarantees, and so on. By putting your decoy offers and premium offers side-by-side, leads can see how much more valuable your premium offer is. I like Decoy Offers because they get more customers overall. They either take the decoy version or the premium version. If they take the premium, great. If they take the decoy, also great. It gives you time to upgrade them rather than losing them. But either way, you can close everyone. This makes it cheap and profitable to get new customers. And *any* business can use it.

Here are the steps to make a Decoy Offer:

1) Advertise a lesser, smaller, or simpler version of your premium offer as a decoy.

2) When leads engage, offer both options, but emphasize the premium one.

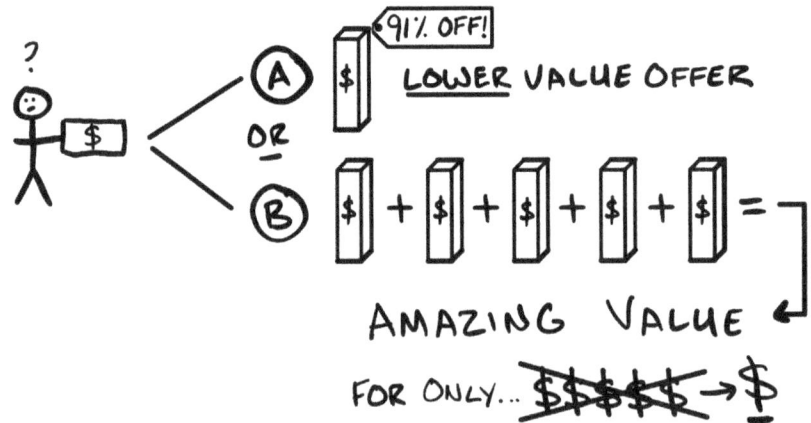

Example:

Float Tank Center (Service)

Attraction Offer: "Free 6-Week Stress Release" **OR** "$6 6-Week Stress Release."

Decoy Option: One float per month with at-home do it yourself stress relief exercises.

Premium Option: Two times per week floats for 6 weeks, 1–1 consulting, journal, sleep routine. Satisfaction guaranteed.

Gym Offer (Local Business)

Attraction Offer: "Free 21-Day Transformation" **OR** "$21 21-Day Transformation."

Decoy Option: Workouts done in a Skool.com group once a day. A general nutrition plan. Can watch recordings. No support. No guarantee.

Premium Option: Unlimited workouts, a personalized nutrition plan, 1–1 accountability, results guaranteed (or you get another 21 days free).

Important Notes

How To Make Your Decoy Offer. Offer fewer components, older models, or less personalized versions of your premium offer. Also, remove any guarantees. Your Attraction Offer only has to get leads to engage. Nothing more.

Advertise Benefits Not The Features. We want to sell them on the dream outcome. We advertise a *transformation* in 21 days, not workouts and meal plans. Leads get specific product details in the sales presentation, *not* in the advertising! Private jets and rowboats can both get you to an exotic island, but the premium option is certainly more enjoyable.

You Can Advertise Discounts in Four Ways. Let's say you had a year-long thing that cost $100 per month. If you wanted to let them pay $900 for the year, you could say:

1) Percentage Off: 25% off

2) Absolute Amount: $300 off

3) Free Portion: 3 Months Free

4) The Total Package: One Year For $900 ($1,200)

They all mean the same thing. It's worth testing to see which one converts better in your market.

Make The Contrast Huge. The value of the premium option comes from huge differences with the decoy option. So make the decoy option as basic as reasonable. Then make the premium option as awesome as possible. The bigger the contrast, *the better the deal*, the more customers will take it. Think about adding more features, benefits, bonuses, and guarantees, etc.

Discount Offers Have Higher Show Up Rates Than Free Offers. In my experience, if you run a Free Attraction offer, you'll get more leads. If you run a Discount Offer, you'll get fewer leads, but a higher percentage will show up. So if you have low show up rates for appointments, try a discount offer instead. This is especially important for businesses where you have a high cost of someone not showing up (think doctors, lawyers, dentists, etc).

If Possible, Present The Premium Offer First. In a perfect world, they take the premium offer immediately. The decoy offer stays in your back pocket. If they come in specifically asking for the decoy option up front…

Get Them To Give You Permission To Sell Them. If they ask to hear about your decoy, you are legally required to present it, or you prefer to present it first, here's how I like to do it:

Ask them a simple question: *"Are you here for free stuff or lasting results?"*

And as soon as they say "results," which most people do, skip to your premium offer.

If they say "free stuff," present the decoy offer then immediately contrast it with your premium offer. Then only <u>after</u> presenting <u>both</u>, ask them, *"Which do you think will get you to your goal faster?"* or *"Which would you prefer: XXX less valuable benefit or YYY more valuable benefit 1, 2, 3…?"* At this point, they'll have to say the premium offer. Then you can move forward with the sale, mutually agreeing it's the best thing for them.

When Making Your Premium Offer, *Get Excited About It*. Present it as superior to the decoy offer, because it is. And, assuming it is, how it fits the customer better. Your excitement motivates people to take the options that will give them the most value.

From a selling perspective, you want to talk to the lead as if you already know they will accept your offer. Many salespeople refer to this as an "assumed close." You operate from a position of: *This is what everyone does. This is just a formality. Let me get your ID and credit card so you can get your value.* No hype. Just a friendly disposition. Almost bored over how regularly people buy.

Surprise Benefit (Optional). To take this a step further, if someone takes the decoy option, you can choose to surprise them with a few low/zero cost features from your premium offer. Just say something like, "Hey, I'm gonna throw this in, even though it's part of our premium offer just because I want you to get great results." This builds goodwill, over delivers, and increases the chance they take your upsells later. Remember—they're still leads!

Expect to make money fast. If you're not, then make the contrast between offers larger.

Exercise #3: Create Your Decoy Offer

1. Write down the four ways you could advertise: FREE or DISCOUNT

    a. FREE: _____

    b. % Off: _____

    c. Absolute Amount Off: _____

    d. Portion Free: _____

2. Write down decoy offer and price: _____
   _____

3. Write down your better premium offer and price: _____
   _____

Buy X Get Y Free

Buy one puppy, get two puppies free!

Story

There's this place in Nashville called Boot Factory. It's been there forever, outlasting all the other tourist traps. They've got this massive neon sign with a cowboy boot bigger than a car, and their offer is wild: Buy one pair, get two free.

Now, as a kid, I thought this was nuts. How could they stay in business giving away so much? But years later, with some business savvy under my belt, I went back and it all clicked.

Here's the genius part: They mark up the price of one pair to cover the cost of three. So that "final offer"... for a $600 pair... that actually covers three pairs. But the way they frame it makes it feel like you're getting this insane deal. And people go nuts for it.

Description

In Buy X Get Y Free Offers, when customers buy something, they get other stuff free. The more free stuff they get, and the higher its value, the better it works. Free offers get *way* more attention than discount offers. But if you only have one thing to sell, and you give it away, *you go hungry*. In situations like this, businesses tend to lean on discounts. They run "sales" relying on holidays, seasonal changes, or whatever, as reasons to *temporarily* lower prices and get more customers.

But, by selling more than one thing at once, you can turn Discount Offers into even stronger *Free Offers*. When you have more than one item, you can make the discount value large enough that it covers the price of more stuff. For example, I could sell three t-shirts for $10 each for a total of $30 *or* I could sell one t-shirt for $30 and give two away free. <u>It's the same price, but *way more free stuff*</u>!

And if I wanted to offer a discount (rather than *only* reframe the price), I could do this. I could sell three t-shirts for $6.67 each for a total of $20 (33% discount), *or*, keeping the same discount, I could sell one t-shirt for $20 and give two away free. <u>It's the same price, but *way more free stuff again*</u>!

Boot Factory took the first option. They tripled the price of one pair of boots and added value… in more boots. And an expensive pair of boots with two free pairs gets *Boot Factory* more customers than selling one pair at a fair price. Plus, if you can include *free*, then it'll attract even more customers.

Examples

Buy 1 Get 2 Free Physical Products Offer: (The *Boot Factory* Offer)

- One Pair of Boots: $200
- Buy X Get Y Free Offer: Buy One Pair For $600, Get Two Pairs for Free
- End Result: They still buy three pairs of $200 boots for a total of $600

3 Versions: 18 Months Of Services AKA "3 Pairs Of Boots"

Good: *"Buy 12 Months Get 6 Months Free"* - $1,800

Better: *"Buy 9 Months Get 9 Months Free"* - $1,800

Best: *"Buy 6 Months Get 12 Months Free"* - $1,800

Everyone pays the same price for the same amount of service. <u>But, the third option is the most compelling</u>. (Hint: It has the most free stuff!)

Important Notes

Buy X Get Y Free Gets People To Buy More Stuff *And* Provides More Value.

Raise Prices Before Giving Stuff Away To Preserve Profits. If you use this to attract customers, it will work. And since it will work, you need to make money. So, *permanently* raise prices to accommodate the discount.

Buy X Get Y Free Works Better If You Have More Free Stuff Than Paid Stuff.

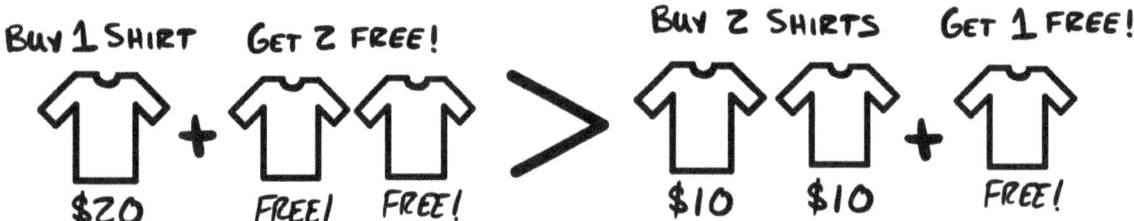

Buy two get one free is not as strong as buy one get two free. To make it work better, give more free than you ask people to buy. Just play with the pricing until it makes sense for you.

The Free Things Can Be Different From The Paid Things

You can mix and match whatever you want. Just make sure the value of the *different* free stuff still makes the offer compelling. Ex.: Let's say socks have a $10 value. If they buy one shirt for $10 but get $20 of free socks, it may seem like a better deal.

More Free Cheaper Things Can Work Better Than Fewer Free Expensive Things.

Let's say I could only afford to give one shirt away for free, but for the same cost I could give them three pairs of socks. I'd probably test "Buy 1 Shirt Get 1 Shirt Free" against "Buy 1 Shirt, Get <u>3</u> Socks Free." Socks cost less than a shirt but people still see "buy <u>one</u> thing get <u>three</u> things free." Sometimes, *more* cheaper things work better than *fewer* expensive things.

Do Not Make Offers Like This If You Can't Manage Money. While Buy X Get Y Free offers create massive cash flow for a business, you need to deliver. So if you get a whole year's worth of payments in a month, *make sure you can deliver* for the whole year.

Make This Offer To Existing Customers For Fast Cash. If you have a recurring business already, and need cash fast, you can make this offer to existing customers. Just cap how many can take the offer to 10% of your customer base.

Even If Customers Prepay Now, You Can Still Upsell Them Different Stuff Later. A lot of people don't want to make more offers to customers who prepay for stuff. This is a mistake. Speaking from experience, these are people who spend the most money. Give them other offers to buy, and they will.

If Customers Only Buy Once, Make The Buy As Big As You Can: If you only have one shot, you may as well make it count!

Exercise #4: Reframe Your Offer as "Free"

Pick one existing offer in your business (product, service, or package). Rewrite it as a *Buy X Get Y Free* offer without changing the total value exchanged. Example: instead of "3 months for $300," try "Buy 1 month, get 2 free."

Write your version below :

Current offer: _____

Reframed offer: _____

Why this framing feels more compelling: _____

Exercise #5: Test the "More Free Than Paid" Rule

List three variations of a *Buy X Get Y Free* idea for your business. Make sure each version gives more free items or time than paid ones. Then, circle the one that would sound most irresistible to your audience.

1. Buy _____ Get _____ Free
2. Buy _____ Get _____ Free
3. Buy _____ Get _____ Free

Chosen offer: _____

Why it wins: _____

_____

FREE GIFT: Buy X Get Y Free Video Course

Buy X Get Y Free get lots of cash and lots of customers. You just need to know your math. I made a free video for you giving a few more creative ways to use it. You can watch the video fo' free at acquisition.com/training/money. Scan the QR code if you hate typing.

Pay Less Now or Pay More Later

Time is money - Benjamin Franklin

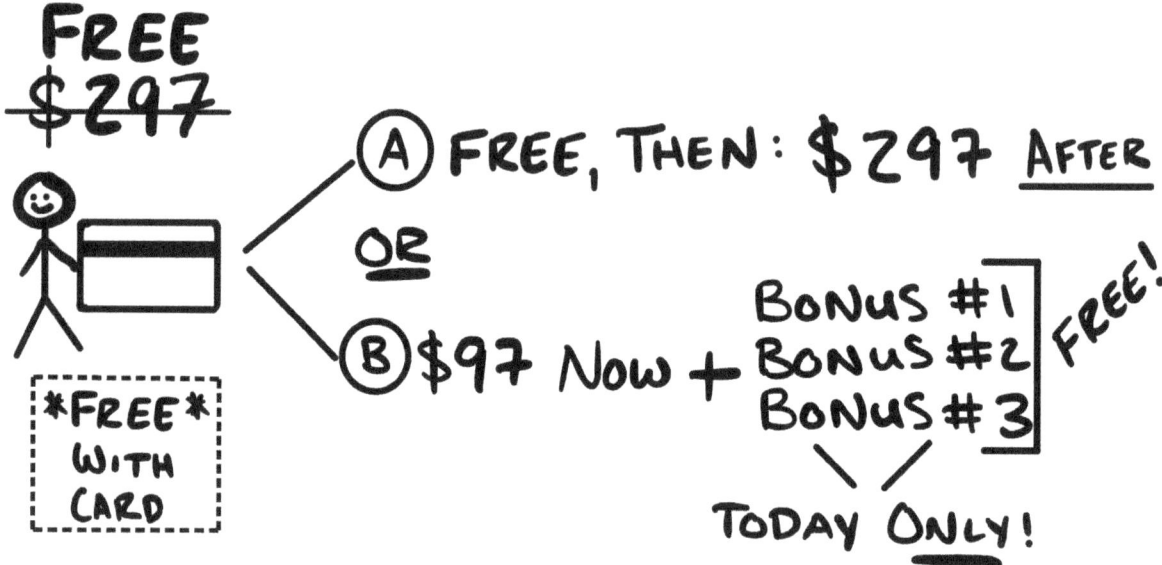

June 2016.

A headline caught my attention: *"Double your reading speed in 3 hours, or it's free."* I opened and scanned the text. Inside, the world's fastest reader offered a free training to double my reading speed in three hours. So, I registered. Why not?

The registration page said, "You can put your credit card down for $0, and get billed $297 tomorrow. And if your reading speed doesn't double, just email us before then and we'll cancel the charge. But you must attend in order to be eligible" <u>or</u> "You can just pay $97 right now, and as a free bonus, get the recordings, which won't be for sale anywhere else."

I decided on the first option. I wanted to see if my reading speed doubled before paying for anything. The whole training I expected him to sell me more stuff. But he simply provided value. After two hours, using his tactics, my reading speed doubled. *Impressive.* The training had been true to the promise. He earned his $297.

After that, he talked about how I could learn to read even faster with his eight-week training program. I was satisfied with my results, so I chose not to take the upsell. He taught me a skill I still use to this day. But, the true value came from learning a brand-new Attraction Offer.

Description

In Pay Less Now or Pay More Later, you give people a choice to pay full-price later OR pay a discounted price now. This play works so well because we remove *all* risk from the customer. They pay later *and* only if they like it. So it combines the benefits of a delayed payment and a satisfaction guarantee. *Anyone can sell this*. Almost anyone will agree to pay later if they are satisfied. But, once they agree to pay later, you can get them to pay *now* with hefty discounts and valuable bonuses.

The *pay later* option allows you to advertise "free" since they can choose to pay or not. This gets lots of leads engaged. But this free offer has an added benefit, *we get their card on file*. If they choose this option and hate the product, then they can cancel any time before the charge goes through.

If they accept the *pay later* option, we make a follow up offer to *pay now*. Pay now options provide a 20–50% discount and greater bonuses. And since we already have their card on file, we make it easy for them to pay.

Whether they choose to *pay now* or *pay later*, you've got customers, and likely, some profit. But, to take full advantage of this offer, you'll want something else to sell. So have something *more, better, newer* to offer when the time is right. In the story, this was the eight-week training course he offered at the end. And don't worry, we go deep on upsells in the next section.

Examples:

Find Your First Real Estate Deal—Free 3-Day Workshop

Pay Later: $0 for 3-day workshop. They get billed $500 at the end unless they cancel.

Pay Now: $299 for 3-day workshop plus recordings, 1–1 call with certified distressed property expert, plus printed materials to use (delivered at the workshop).

Upsell: $30,000 to take you through every other step of closing your first deal within six months *plus*: legal templates, advisor to vet the investment, inspection checklist, etc.

Local Business Service: Trim Your Hedges For Free

Pay Later: $0 Lawn Cut + Hedges then $599 after.

Pay Now: $369 Lawn Cut + Hedges + Lawn Treatment.

Upsell: $199 per month lawncare services.

The rep comes to the house, makes the estimate, and offers both options, then upsells after the work is done.

Physical Products: 14-Day Clothing Trial

Pay Later*: $0 Now. Get it. Then get billed $149 in 14 days.

Pay Now: $97 for the clothing + an accessory that goes with it.

Upsell: The dress comes with an offer for a monthly subscription to more clothes like this.

Customers must return the product in like-new condition before billing to qualify for guarantee.

Important Notes

Promise A Clear Yes/No Result. First, make your promise a clear "yes or no" result. Second, make sure you can deliver on it within your time frame. If you don't, they will ask not to be billed. Keep the promise simple, clear, and measurable. This avoids unnecessary cancellations.

Make a Conditional Satisfaction Guarantee. *People can only cancel the billing if they qualify.* Be sure to track the conditions necessary to qualify. Think: attendance, showing up to an appointment, turning in data, etc. Make the criteria what people do to get the most value out of the product.

Optimizing Your "Pay Now" And "Pay Later" Offer. If too many people take your "pay later" option, discount the "pay now" option more, add better bonuses, or both. If too many people take your "pay now" option, do the opposite.

- The *Pay Later* option has a delayed payment with a conditional guarantee.
    - Have clear criteria to qualify for the guarantee and easy ways to measure it.
    - If you can, align the criteria with what gets people the most value from the product.
- The *Pay Now* option offers a 20–50% discount and bonuses *if they pay now.*
    - Offer customers the *pay now* option after they accept the *pay later* option.
    - If they choose *pay now*, they get the discount and bonuses *instead of* the guarantee.

If More Than 10% Of "Pay Later" People Cancel Their Payment. You promised too much, the guarantee conditions are too low, or the price is too high. <u>Note</u>: No matter how well you deliver, *some* people will cancel their payment. That's okay. Factor it in your costs of doing business. Give extra attention to those who claim they haven't received what was promised before the cancellation deadline.

This Also Works For Recurring Revenue Businesses. You just give them the option to pay a higher ongoing rate 30 days later, *or* they pay less today and keep the lower rate for good. Plus, add in some bonuses. See *Section V: Continuity Offers Chapter: Continuity Bonus Offers*, for more details.

Exercise #6: Create Your Pay Less Now Pay More Later Offer

Use the template below to sketch your own version of this offer structure. Make sure the "Pay Later" version includes a conditional guarantee, and the "Pay Now" version includes a discount and bonuses.

Product/Service : _____

Pay Later Offer: _____

Pay Now Offer: _____

Guarantee Condition (e.g. attendance, usage): _____

_____

Exercise #7: Identify a Clear Yes/No Promise

Write one simple, measurable result your product or service could promise that can be clearly tracked during a free or trial period. Make sure it's a "yes" or "no" outcome.

Before: _____

After: _____

How I'll measure success (metric or condition): _____

_____

FREE GIFT: Pay Less Now Pay More Later Training [No Opt-in]

This is one of the most creative offers I've ever seen or used. It does exceptionally well with digital products and short duration services. These can be scary effective and also "feel good." It's super easy to teach salesmen as well. If you want to learn more about them I made a deeper training for you free at acquisition.com/training/money. Scan the QR code for easy fast access.

Free Goodwill Offer

He who said money can't buy happiness hasn't given enough away.

"I became a quadriplegic in 2018 and was living on welfare until I found your content and book… I made $50,000 the following 12 months as a freelancer." - Danny W.

I have a question for you…

Would you help someone you've never met if it cost you nothing, but you didn't get credit?

Most people do, in fact, judge a book by its cover. So here's my ask on behalf of a struggling entrepreneur you've never met: **Please help that entrepreneur by leaving this book a review. Your review helps…**

…one more small business like Bill's provide for their community. In Bill's own words: *"I opened a pizzeria in early 2022 shortly after finding $100M Offers. Sales started slow, but we did it! After I read $100M Leads we implemented many things like having customers donate to the local food bank for a chance to win free pizza for a year. I've lost count of how many new customers we've gotten after doing these things for the community. This absolutely proves this stuff works for any type of business. Thank you!"* - Bill T.

…one more entrepreneur like Thomas support their family. In Thomas's own words: *"After ten years, I got laid off from my 9-5 job. But then I found your book and opened a tour guide business in Colorado. Fast forward two years and we have five employees! I literally took what I learned and built my dream. Now my kids and wife are happier than ever."*

…one more employee like Miguel's have more meaningful work. In Miguel's own words: *"I received the book as a gift and decided to pass it on to my six employees. Since then, our business has undergone a remarkable transformation and continues to grow on a monthly basis. Not only that, but I also gave it to my independent contractor trainers. Thank you."*

If you tell yourself you'll do it later, instead, please do it now. It takes fewer than 60 seconds to change someone's life forever.

If you are on Audible - hit the three dots in the top right of your device, click rate & review, then leave a few sentences about the book with a star rating.

If you are reading on Kindle or an e-reader - scroll to the bottom of the book, then swipe up and it will prompt a review for you.

If for some reason these changed - you can go to Amazon (or wherever you purchased this) and leave a review right on the book's page.

If you feel good about helping a faceless entrepreneur, you are my kind of people. Welcome to #mozination. You're one of us.

I'm that much more excited to help you make more money than you can possibly imagine. You'll love the tactics I'm about to share in the coming chapters. Thank you from the bottom of my heart. Now, back to our regularly scheduled programming.

- Your biggest fan, Alex

Exercise #8: Please Leave a Review If This Helped You

Please leave a review for this workbook and summary so other entrepreneurs can find it (if you deem it worthy of their time). :)

Attraction Conclusion

Extra! Extra! Hear All About It!

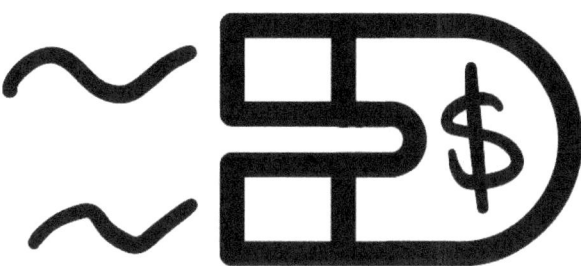

The point of Attraction offers is to turn strangers into customers. And, do it in a way that gets more cash up front. Ideally, we get enough cash to cover the cost of the customer and the cost to deliver our thing *multiple times over*. That way we can pay ourselves back *and* get our next customer.

I showed you the five most powerful Attraction Offers I've seen and used: Win Your Money Back, Giveaways, Decoy Offers, Buy X Get Y Free, and Pay Less Now or Pay More Later. I've applied them at one time or another to every business I own.

After using Attraction Offers, we've got more customers. And now that we got 'em, we need to boost our 30-day profits by selling them more stuff. This leads us to the next component of a $100M Money Model—Upsell Offers: *What to offer next*.

Exercise #9: Pick Your Attraction Offer

1. Pick the attraction offer you will start with:

    a. Win Your Money Back ( )

    b. Giveaways ( )

    c. Decoy Offers ( )

    d. Buy X Get Y Free ( )

    e. Pay Less Now or Pay More Later ( )

2. Refer to your exercise answers from this chapter and get started.

SECTION III: UPSELL OFFERS

Do you want fries with that? - McDonald's Famous Upsell

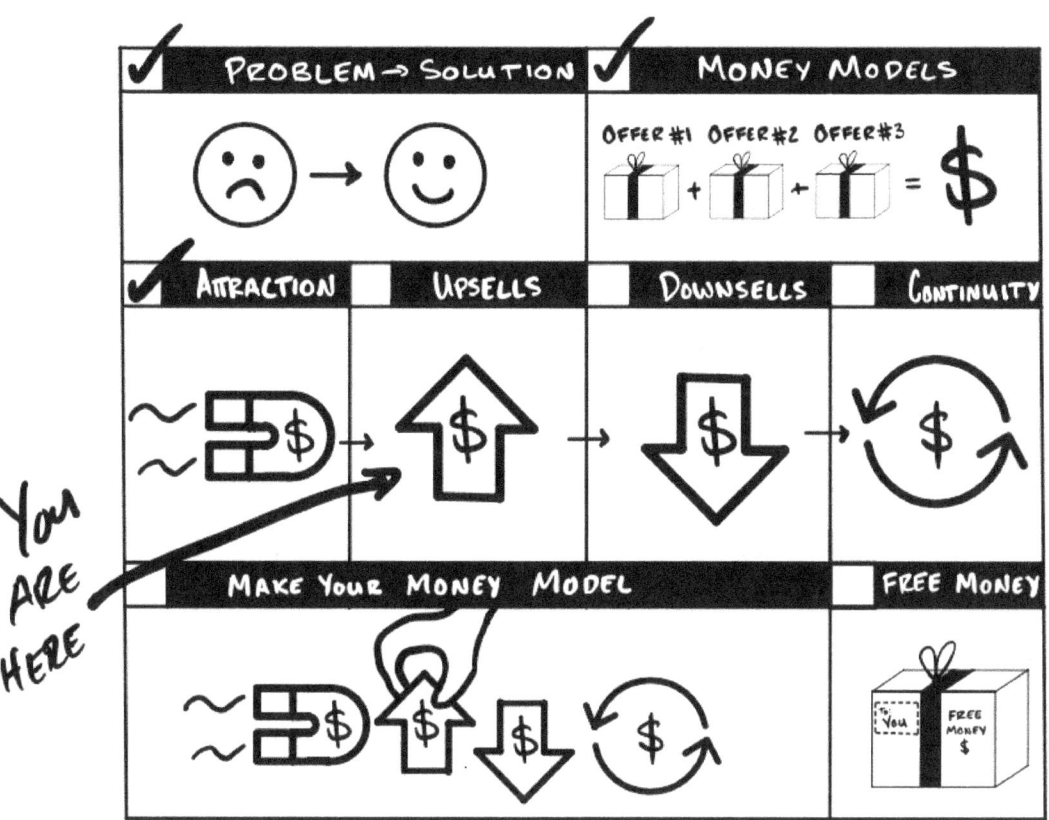

How Upsells Work

When an offer solves a problem, another appears. You *upsell* the solution to the problem your offer reveals. Often, upsells make the majority of the profit. They make or break a Money Model.

Let's say a burger shop makes $0.25 in profit on a $2.00 burger. If it was the only offer they had, they'd have to sell ~10,000 burgers a day to cover costs and *barely* eke out a "living."

But, they have more offers beyond just the burger. They ask *"Do you want fries with that?"* If they say yes, they profit another $0.75 and ask *"Do you want to make it a meal?"* which adds a drink. If someone says yes, they profit an *extra* $1.75. Their profit goes from $0.25 to $2.00—*an 8x increase.* And on top of that, they offer a third upsell: *"Do you want to supersize your meal for just a buck more?"* This takes profit from a measly $0.25 to a massive $3—*an 11.6x increase.* And now this little burger place actually has a chance at succeeding.

BURGER, FRIES $ SODA METHOD

OLD WAY
- PRICE: $2.00
- COST: $1.75
- PROFIT: .25

NEW WAY
- PRICE: $2.00
- COST: $1.75
- PROFIT: .25

+ MEDIUM (8x Gross Profit/Sale)
- UPSELL PRICE: $2.00
- UPSELL COST: $.25
- NEW PROFIT: $1.75

+ LARGE (11.6x Gross Profit/Sale)
- UPSELL PRICE: $1.00
- UPSELL COST: $.10
- NEW PROFIT: .90

I show this basic (and common!) example to point *out* one thing—your first offer *doesn't always* make the profit. In other words, *the thing you sell the most isn't always the thing you make the most profit on.* You make it on the second, third, and in the case of the burger business, fourth offers and beyond. If McDonald's didn't upsell fries and soda, there wouldn't be a McDonald's. If you want to win, you have to figure out your version of *"Do you want fries with that?"* If you don't, others will.

Upsells fail when:

- You offer something they don't want (too different or doesn't solve their problem)
- You offer it at the wrong time (before they've experienced the problem)
- You offer it the wrong way (they don't believe you)
- Or, a combination of the above.

In summary, Upsells tend to offer:

- *More* of what they just got (think quantity) - *Why have one burger when you can have two?*

- *Better* versions of it (think quality) - *Why have mystery meat when you can have sirloin?*

- *New* or complementary stuff (think different) - *Do you want fries and a soda with that burger?*

I Use Four Simple And Brutally Effective Upsell Offers:

- The Classic Upsell
- Menu Upsells
- Anchor Upsells
- Rollover Upsells

And with just a few tweaks, you can fit them into your business today.
Warning: This section is brutally effective and must be used ethically. That being said, let's make some money.

The Classic Upsell

You Can't Have X Without Y!

Summer 2016.

I sat down in a swanky restaurant with a childhood mentor who was a fourth-generation furrier. He started by breaking down how overpriced the food was. The conversation transitioned and he brought up that I was "in the game now." We started talking about how he had invented "summer storage" for fur coats and made millions every year with it. He excitedly told me their new money model:

"We advertise free earmuffs with coat storage. And get this. When customers come to get their muffs and store their coats he says, *'Great. And we'll store those as well for $30. You don't want to store anything else do you?'* And, of course, they say no."

"Wait a second, so you get them to pay for additional storage for the free ear muffs by getting them to say no?"

He taught me how he upsold customers into storing their free earmuffs by saying *no* they didn't want to store anything *else*. This is called an assumed close, which we'll cover in a second.

Description

The Classic Upsell offers a solution to the customer's next problem *the moment* they become aware of it. I explain the Classic Upsell first because it's extremely profitable, easy, and anyone can do it. Main reason: current customers *always* have a higher chance of buying your stuff than strangers. And, when timed right, customers upsell themselves.

The Classic Upsell relies on knowing more about your customer's problem than they do. The idea is simple: your core offer solves one problem and creates another. *Your upsell immediately solves that next problem.* This gives the classic upsell its "You can't have X without Y" structure. Like the rental car story. You can't have a car without insurance. You can't have a car without gas. You can't have a good trip without a late checkout. Etc. And all of these things become immediately apparent *as soon as* the customer makes the first purchase.

Bottom Line: If a problem appears, and you can solve it immediately—in exchange for money—*do it!*

Examples

Local Car Wash Service

First purchase: Car Wash

Upsell: Sealant

You're not gonna wanna do the wash without sealant. You get way more for your money.

Physical Product

First Purchase: Bicycle

Upsell #1: Helmet

Upsell #2: Lights

Upsell #3: Puncture-Resistant Tires

You can't have a bike without a helmet!

Digital Product

First purchase: Course on Exercising

Upsell: Nutrition Course

You can't out-exercise a bad diet… so you're gonna want our course on nutrition.

Important Notes

Actually Do It. You'd be amazed how many businesses come to me and only sell one thing.

Offer More Profitable Upsells First. If I offer two products and one has a higher profit than the other, I offer the higher profit option first.

Get Them To "Say No To Say Yes." People are trained to say "no" in response to "You don't want anything else, do you?" But this actually turns a "no" into a "yes." So when upselling, the question translates to: *You don't want anything [besides what I just offered] do you?*

Surprise And Delight. Let's say you have four bonuses you save to add to get people to buy who are on the fence. Add one at a time. If they say yes before you add them, still give them all four. It will surprise and delight them.

Sell More When They're Buying More—Hyper Buying Cycle. Most buyers enter a "hyper buying" cycle when they decide to do something new. This is when they spend a huge chunk of money in a short period of time. Think weddings, starting new hobbies, having babies, moving to new places, and so on.

Use Free Bonuses To Create Problems Upsell Offers Solve. Bonuses solve problems. And because of the problem-solution cycle, they can also reveal them. Upsells can solve that new problem.

The Faster People Get Access To Stuff, The More They'll Value It. A $10,000 thing you get later is worth less than a $10,000 thing you get now. The longer it takes someone to access something, the less value it has in the moment. So if you want to raise the chance of them taking the upsell, make it available as soon as you can. Bonus points if you put it in their hands before they've said yes. It's way harder to give something back than it is to say no.

If You Bundle Upsells, Name Them. It's easier to sell someone one thing than nine things. By bundling items together, you can make one "ask" and get nine sales. I name the packages based on customer type *and/or* result. For example, "Fastest results" bundle or "Transformation package" or "Minimum package."

Integrate Upsells Into Your Other Offers. Make stuff you upsell part of how you deliver other offers. Then, more customers will take them. Integrate the next thing you wanna sell into the first thing they buy.

Make Sure You Book-A-Meeting-From-A-Meeting (BAMFAM). The more times you can upsell, the more people you will upsell. If you upsell more people, you make more money. Since you want that… end every appointment by scheduling the next appointment. So if you agree to meet again, *agree on why and when right then*.

Upsell As Many Times As It Makes Sense To. Offer as many solutions as there are problems you can solve. Don't be shy. If you can solve it, offer to. The second worst thing that happens is they say no. *The worst thing is if they would've said yes but you never asked.*

Upsell Guarantees, Warranties, and Insurance. Many businesses offer guarantees on products. Many businesses offer warranties on products. Many businesses offer insurance on products. You can upsell all of them. *So instead of doing it for free, just add 5–50% onto the price in exchange for a guarantee that your thing does what you say it will.* Ex.: An art studio used to replace damaged portraits at no charge. I told them to start asking customers if they would pay an extra 10% for it. Now, 30% of customers buy a warranty the art studio used to give away for free. Pure profit.

Exercise #10: Design Your Classic "You Can't Have X Without Y" Upsell

Start with one of your main offers. Identify the immediate, logical problem it creates. Then write the upsell that solves that new problem.

Main Offer : _____

Immediate Problem It Creates: _____

Upsell Offer (Solves That Problem): _____

How You'd Frame It: "You can't have [X] without [Y]"

Exercise #11: Create a Bundle + Downsell Path

Bundle together 2–4 related upsells into a named package. Then identify one item you can "peel off" as a downsell if they hesitate.

Bundle Name: _____

What's Included: _____

Peel-off Downsell Option: _____

Framing Idea: "Would you prefer to start with just [X]?"

Menu Upsells

You don't need that… you need this.

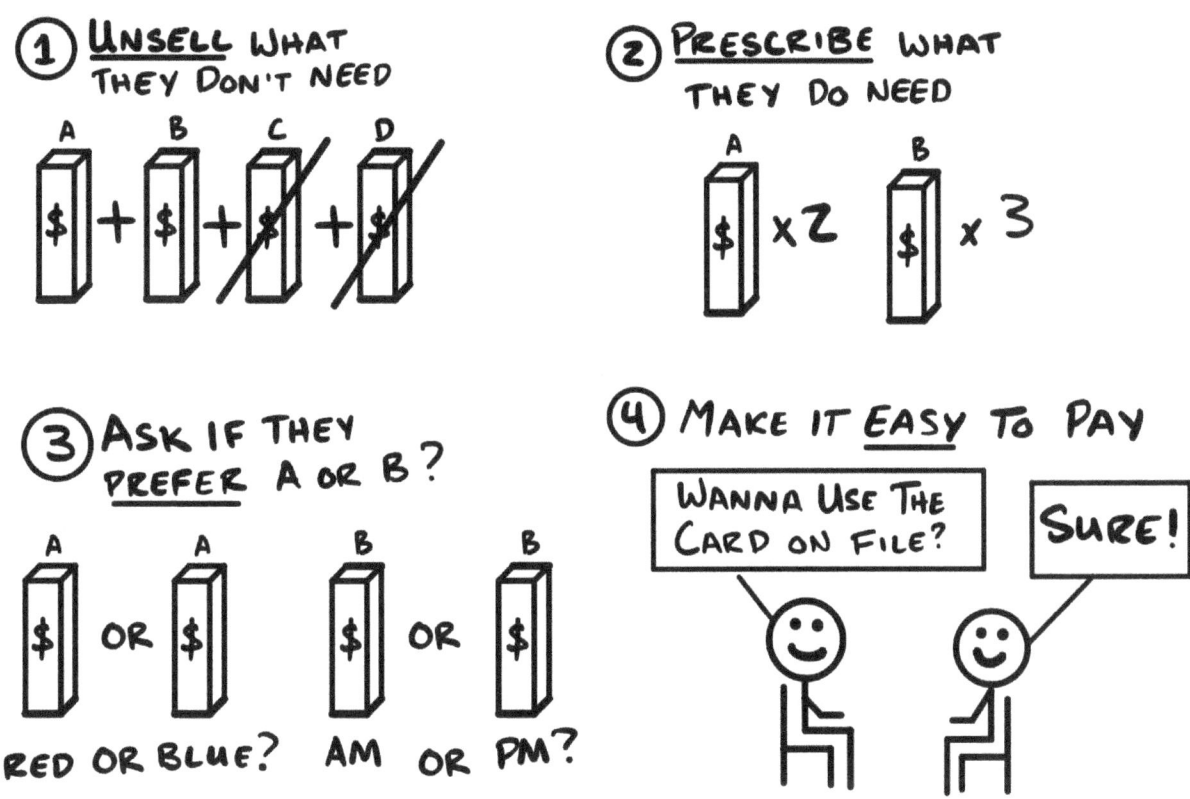

December 2013.

I struggled to sell supplements at my gym, despite trying various tactics like keeping shelves stocked and explaining the science. On a particularly rough day, after 19 failed nutrition consults, I was desperate to make a sale to my 20th client. In my nervousness, I forgot my script and simply asked the client to choose between flavors, which unexpectedly led to a sale. I continued this approach, also asking if they wanted to use the card on file, and ended up selling to the next 20 customers in a row.

Takeaway: I stumbled on two tactics that changed my upsell game forever. First, the A/B Upsell—I ask *which product they prefer* rather than *whether* they want the product at all. Second, asking *if they want to use the card on file* rather than asking them to take out their card again. I still use both to this day.

August 2014.

After mastering my initial sales technique, I was consistently selling $5,000 to $10,000 worth of supplements per month. One day, a customer's relentless questions led me to write out detailed instructions, which unexpectedly became a powerful sales tool. By incorporating written instructions into my sales process and assuming the sale, I dramatically increased my profits without needing to spend extra time on each customer.

Takeaway: I learned that *detailed* and *personalized* instructions upsell more people than vague and general suggestions. I call this prescription upselling.

November 2016.

I had gotten really good at selling supplements during gym launches—so good that I kept running out of stock. One day, a customer came in asking for products I'd already sold out of. Without thinking, I did something different: I started "unselling." I recommended cheaper alternatives that would work just as well and even crossed items off her list that she didn't actually need. Her reaction surprised me. Instead of being disappointed, she seemed relieved and grateful. My honest approach—telling her what she *shouldn't* buy and focusing only on what would help her—built instant trust. Even though I'd eliminated half her list and downgraded the rest, she still bought from me. More importantly, she felt good about it.

That's when I realized something powerful: sometimes the best way to sell is to unsell. Later, I even started keeping certain products in stock just so I could cross them out in front of customers. It sounds backwards, but that single act of removing something they didn't need created enough goodwill that they'd trust my recommendations on what they *did* need.

Takeaway: I call this process unselling.

Description

In a Menu Upsell, you tell customers which options they don't need. Then, tell them what they do need, their preferences, *and* how to get their value from it. Menu Upsells combine up to four tactics: A/B Upselling, Prescription Upselling, Unselling, and Card on File.

First, I unsell what customers don't need.

Second, I prescribe what they do need.

Third, I ask their preferences between A and B.

Last, I make buying easy by asking if they want to use the card on file.

Unselling. You unsell by telling customers what they don't need so that you can emphasize what they do. Here, instead of asking *if* they want to buy it or not, you explain **what they don't need** as a way to **get them excited about what they do.** Unsells vary based on the customer's needs. When some options work best, you can cross out the rest. After telling them what they don't need…

Prescription Upsell. We tell them what they do need. Prescription Upsells work well when offering a choice is inconvenient and you have only one thing that solves the problem. Prescription upselling has two important components. First, you have to explain how it integrates with offers they already bought. Second, you personalize and detail how to maximize its value. Here, instead of asking *if* they want to buy it or not, you explain **how to use it** as if they already have. Again, we remove the option of not buying to lower the chance they don't buy. And once I have told them exactly how they're going to use everything…

A/B Upsell. We ask them their preferences. A/B Upsells work for *multiple offers that solve the same problem*. You make A/B Upsells by asking their preference. Instead of asking *if* customers wanted to buy a product, yes or no, we ask which product they **prefer**: A or B. Either choice results in an upsell. Basically, when you give people the option to not buy, some don't buy. So, I give the option to pick between buying two similar things. Once they know what they're buying and how they're gonna use it, I suggest the easiest way for them to pay…

Card on File. A cherry on top of all this upsell goodness. I literally ask, "Do you want to use the card on file?" Here, instead of asking *if* they want to pay or not, you **refer** to ways they already have. This gets more people to buy because it lowers the "hidden costs" of buying. Picking which card to use. Taking it out. Being reminded of ugly buying decisions in the past. Even the hassle of buying stuff in a rush… and who knows how many more. Just know if you make it easy for people to buy, more people will.

This took me ten years to learn. May you get the same value in ten minutes.

Examples

Massage Therapist

Unsell: We have a lymphatic massage available, but you're not pregnant or just out of surgery right? So we can cross that out.

Prescribe: Since your shoulder hurts, we'll heat you up first, then hit your trigger points, and after that, we'll do some dynamic stretches.

A/B: So would you rather do it before work or on the way home?

Card On File: Wanna just use the card on file?

Dog Food

Unsell: You're not gonna need this small bag or this puppy stuff—you've got a big dog! You don't need these vitamins either because the food already contains them.

Prescribe: You're also gonna wanna give your dog one of these joint chews at each meal. And every 90 days, give them one of these wafers for heartworms. Also, make sure to bring him back next month. Let's get that booked now.

A/B: So does your dog prefer beef or chicken flavor?

Card On File: Wanna just use the card on file?

Digital Product

Unsell: You don't need all eight courses yet. You just need to solve X, Y, & Z. Tell ya what. I'll send you some free stuff that'll solve problems X and Y. Then, you'll just need one course for problem Z…

Prescribe: But to solve Z, you're definitely gonna wanna do the course *this* particular way. Can you put an hour a day towards it? Okay—great. This will prevent any other Z problems cropping up later.

A/B: Would you rather have direct message or phone support? Okay great. And would you like to start today or Monday?

Card On File: Awesome. Wanna just use the card on file?

Important Notes:

Make Anything A/B Sellable. You can turn *anything* into an A/B offer. Just to give you a few ideas… Quantity (do you want one bottle or two?), start dates (start tomorrow or Monday?), payment preference (cash or card?), flavors (chocolate or vanilla?), time slots (morning or afternoon?), media (read or listen?), delivery speeds (standard or overnight?), sizes (small or medium?), colors (black or white?), materials (paper or plastic?), personnel (John or Sara?), communication (call or text?). With some creativity, you can make *anything* an A/B upsell.

If You Make An A/B Offer, Add A Nudge. If your customers have limited experience with your products or services, give them a nudge. "*This is my favorite*" or "*X is usually a safe bet*" or "*A lot of people love this*" or "*Tuesdays sessions are a little smaller if you like that*" or "*Amy does great with high schoolers.*" These one-liners really help move sales along. (Hint: If you want to move one particular product faster, *nudge* that one more.)

If You've Sold Out Of It, Take Payment And Delay Delivery. Later I learned I could just sell them stuff, order it, and set the expectation of when it will arrive. This allowed me to sell way more selection because I didn't have to carry inventory. If you run out, consider just collecting the cash and changing the delivery expectations. You'd be surprised how well this works.

Employees Love Unselling. Employees often *like* helping customers "game the system." *Let them.* Encourage employees to help customers game the system on purpose. Your employees have inside knowledge, so allow them to show customers how to get the most value out of what you have to offer. Everyone wins.

Exercise #12: Build Your Menu Upsell

- Write out what you will *Unsell*: _____
- Write out what you will *Prescribe*: _____
- Write out your *A Offer*: _____
  B Offer: _____
  o Which will you nudge (A or B ?)
- Write out when you will get the card so you can use the *card on file* close: _____

Anchor Upsell

The only thing worse than making a $1,000 offer to a person with a $100 budget…
is making a $100 offer to someone with a $1,000 budget.

2016. After Starting Gym Launch, But Before Making Money.

After starting Gym Launch, I decided to buy a suit to look more professional, budgeting $500 for the purchase. At the suit shop, I tried on a $16,000 suit first, which left me feeling embarrassed and out of place when I saw the price tag. The owner, noticing my discomfort, quickly offered a $2,200 suit, which seemed reasonable in comparison, and I ended up spending $2,500 in total. Looking back, I realized the owner had skillfully used a Price Anchor technique, making the $2,200 suit seem like a bargain compared to the $16,000 one, causing me to spend five times my original budget while feeling satisfied with the purchase.

Description

If you present a premium version that's 5x–10x the price first, lots of people will say no. Then, when you present your main offer, it looks like a *much better deal*. So, more people will buy it.

Anchor Upsells work best when the lower-price offer has the same *core functions* as the premium one. For instance, I didn't care about the designer that much. I just needed a suit. So, compared to the $16,000 suit, the $2,200 suit was a *way better deal*.

Anchor Upsells also have two amazing bonuses. First, anchored customers spend more than they normally would. Second, *some customers still buy the super expensive thing*.

Here are the steps:

1) Present the Anchor - the really expensive thing.

2) Get "The Gasp" - expect the customer to freak out about the cost.

3) Come to the rescue - ask if they care about *what makes it premium*.

4) Present your Main Offer - expect the customer to feel relieved and see the *better deal*.

5) Ask how they wanna pay - *Which card do you prefer?*

Examples

Local Service: Lawn Care

Premium Anchor: Get my cell phone number, fancy mulch, natural pest control, bi-weekly yard maintenance—$1,000 per week

Main Offer: Get my team's number, generic mulch, normal pest control, bi-weekly yard maintenance—$200 per week

Physical Product: A Painting

Premium Anchor: Super protective packaging + 20 year insurance + gift wrapped = $1,000

Main Offer: Normal packaging + 1 year insurance + sticker = $200

Digital Product: Newsletter

Premium Anchor: All previous issues + new issues + 24hrs early = $199/mo

Main Offer: New issues only + on time = $19/mo

Important Notes

If You Treat The Anchor Like A Fake, So Will The Customer. For this to work, you need to actually sell it and they have to actually consider it. Only after they pause, hesitate, or ask for something else, do you move to the next thing. Don't just go through the motions, or it won't work.

Make A Premium Offer You Actually Want People To Buy. Actually present your premium offer like you *want* people to take it. The best way to do that is make it expensive enough you'd be happy they bought it. And if they don't, you still anchored them.

A Proper Anchor Gets "The Gasp." When you do an anchor upsell correctly, customers will have mini panic attacks. I call this "The Gasp." The bigger the gasp, the more they buy.

Once You Get The Gasp—Come To The Rescue. Have the backup thing ready to offer when they gasp. And if they don't gasp… go for the monster sale!

To Get More People To Buy Your Main Offer, Make It A Better Deal. Only tweak a few features from your premium offer to make your main offer. Every offer has features. Some features matter more than others. You want the primary features to stay the same. Fewer people care about secondary features, *so change those*. After anchoring, offering the primary features for ⅕ the price makes the main offer a *great deal*.

Exercise #13: Create Your Anchor Upsell

1. Write out your anchor *(ultra premium)* offer price (5x–10x+) : _____

    a. Anchor Offer PRIMARY Component # 1:

    _____

    b. Anchor Offer PRIMARY Component # 2:

    _____

    c. Anchor Offer SECONDARY Component # 3:

    _____

    d. Anchor Offer SECONDARY Component # 4:

    _____

2. Write out your main offer with *minorly* different secondary components:

    a. Core Offer Price ($\frac{1}{5}^{th}$–$\frac{1}{10}^{th}$ Anchor Price): _____

    b. Core Offer PRIMARY Component # 1: (SAME)

    c. Core Offer PRIMARY Component # 2: (SAME)

    d. Core Offer SECONDARY Component # 3 *(different from anchor offer above)*: _____

    _____

    e. Core Offer SECONDARY Component # 4 *(different from anchor offer above)*: _____

Rollover Upsell

Wanna just roll it forward?

June 2014.

I had been running a successful "Win Your Money Back" offer at my gym, but struggled with a lack of recurring revenue as winners often left after their free months. My friend Justin seemed to be doing much better with a similar offer, so I visited him to investigate. The key difference was that Justin "rolled over" the winnings into a year-long membership, giving winners $50 off per month for a year instead of a lump sum refund or lump sum credit. This approach ensured immediate recurring revenue and longer customer retention, revealing the missing link in my Money Model and solving my cash flow problem.

Description

Rollover Upsells credit some or all of a customer's previous purchases toward your next offer. And this—in my experience—gets *way more* people to take it. So once I know how much credit to give, I figure out three things: *who* to upsell, *what* to upsell, and *how* to roll over the credit.

<u>For the *who*</u>, I use Rollover Upsells in four situations:

First, to re-engage customers who left a while ago.

Second, to rescue upset customers as a better alternative to a refund.

Third, to "rescue" *other people's* upset customers.

Fourth, to upsell regular customers.

<u>For the</u> *what*. Remember, you can upsell *more of what they just got*, *something better*, or *something new and different*. To make money: roll their credit over to something more expensive.

<u>For the</u> *how*, you can apply all or part of the discount up front or spread it over time.

Examples of Rollover Upsells

Chiropractor: *Re-engage old patients with a "Winback" Campaign*

<u>Who</u>: Customers With Six Months Since Last Purchase <u>What</u>: New Plan <u>How</u>: Up front

Reach out to your old patients. Look at their purchase history. Offer to apply some or all of their past purchases towards something more expensive than what they bought.

Ex: *"Hi Mrs. Banks, I wanted to give you your money back, do you have a minute? Great, yea. I wanted to see how your back pain is going? Oh, I'm sorry to hear that. Well, I have some good news. As a way of saying thank you, I want to give you $500 of your money back as credit towards staying pain-free for good. Is that of any interest? Great… let's get you in…"*

Dentist: *Save Your Own Upset Customer With Rollover Upsell*

<u>Who</u>: Upset Customer <u>What</u>: Teeth Whitening <u>How</u>: Front Load $200 Credit.

The person pays $200 for teeth cleaning but doesn't think their teeth got whiter. We explain they need more to get more and upsell into a teeth whitening package which includes multiple sessions, an at-home kit, and multiple deep cleanings. You offer to credit the $200 they paid for the cleaning towards the whitening package.

Software: *Rescue (*Cough* Steal) Other People's Upset Customers*

<u>Who</u>: Competitors' customers <u>What</u>: Service agreement <u>How</u>: Rollover cost to break old agreement.

You find competitors' upset customers and credit the customers' old purchases with them towards a new purchase with you. Roll over the amount they owe with them as credit towards a longer agreement with you.

Ex: *"Hi John, I saw your negative review on their product and it really upset me. To make it up to you, I'll credit whatever payments you have left with them to switch to ours. This way, you don't lose a thing and you start getting the benefits now. Fair enough?"*

Membership: *Spread First Purchase Over a Term*

<u>Who</u>: Current customers <u>What</u>: 12-month membership <u>How</u>: Spread out first purchase.

Somebody buys a small block of service or membership time. As soon as they do, you can offer to apply the entire amount towards more time—like 12 months. I can do the rollover upsell at any time, I just prefer to do it right then. When you do, you take the first purchase's cost and apply it as a discount over the longer agreement. For example, a $600 first purchase makes a $50 per month rollover discount for 12 months.

Important Notes

Use Rollover Offers To Attract New Customers. For example, you roll over some or all of what customers paid another business *towards your thing*. You can find leads for this by scraping contact information from negative product reviews wherever you find them.

Do Rollover Upsells *Before* Refunding. If you did a bad job (hey, it happens), roll over for a "do over." And if they want something different, roll over their purchase toward that thing instead.

Previous Customers Are Still Customers. Upsell Them. Reach out to old customers (6+ months since last purchase). Look at how much they paid before. Decide how much you're willing to roll over. Offer it. I call these "winback campaigns."

Add Urgency To Rollover Upsells. Make Them One Time Only. Optional—make the moment you present the offer the time to take it. *They don't get to sleep on it.* So if they want the credit, they've gotta take it *now*. If not, no big deal. They can still pay full price later.

How To Price Your Rollover Upsell. To make money on a discounted offer, you must have profit left after you discount it. Since I prefer to make a profit, I try to make the upsell offer at least four times more than their rollover credit. So even if I apply the whole amount of the first purchase, it discounts 25% *at most*. Remember, the rules of discounting apply. Bigger discounts make you less profit per sale, but they get more sales.

You Don't Need To Credit The Entire Amount Of Their First Purchase. You can roll over as much or as little of the first purchase you choose. I roll over whatever amount I think would incentivize them to buy the next thing. Test to find the sweet spot.

My "Famous" Gift Card Play. You can use the Rollover Upsell as an Attraction Offer for new *and* current customers by advertising gift cards for 90%+ off. Ex: $200 Gift Cards for $20. Limit them to two per customer and say *they can only use them on other people*. They buy them as gifts and give them to their friends. This makes it a great holiday offer.

When customers buy the gift card, ask them who they want to make it out to and if they'll make an introduction. Then, when their friend comes in, roll over their gift card value towards a bigger offer. Make the *value* of the gift card 20% of the price of whatever you want to sell next. In our example, we sell a $200 gift card for $20. Then, apply that $200 value to an offer with at least a $1,000 price tag. People pay you to refer their friends. It's pretty great. Plus, you get some pocket change from unused gift cards.

Exercise #14: Build Your Rollover Upsell

Choose one product or service your customer recently bought. Now define how you'll credit that toward a more expensive next offer.

Previous Purchase: _____

Rollover Credit Amount: _____

Next Offer (more, better, or new - *aim for 4x the price of above*):

_____

How you'll apply the credit (upfront or spread out): _____

_____

Circle who you will offer it to first: Circle which

a. Past Customers "Win Back" Campaign

b. Current Customers

c. Competitors' Customers "Win Them Over" Campaign

d. New Customers

FREE GIFT: Rollover Upsell Training

This is the upsell I use most frequently. It has elegant urgency built in + goodwill. I made a video for you going over some of the scripting so you can see me do it. It's free. No opt-in required. Watch it at acquisition.com/training/money. I put a QR code for easy fast access.

Upsell Offers Conclusion

Solve rich people problems, they pay better.

Anytime you offer something *next*, you upsell. Upsells play a key role in Money Models by getting more cash from customers *faster* than you otherwise would have. And if your Attraction Offer already covers the costs of getting customers and delivering—*more money ain't a bad thing.*

I showed you the four most powerful Upsells I use: The Classic Upsell, Menu Upsells, Anchor Upsells, and Rollover Upsells. They are core to my business success. Upsells change everything. Many businesses go from burning cash to printing it—*overnight*.

But, sometimes, *people say no.* This leads us to the next component of a $100M Money Model—Downsell Offers: *what to do when they say no…*

Exercise #15: Pick Your Upsell

1. Pick the upsell offer you will start with (check a box below):
    a. The Classic Upsell ( )
    b. Menu Upsell ( )
    c. Anchor Upsell ( )
    d. Rollover Upsell ( )
2. Refer to your exercise answers from this chapter, and start upselling.

SECTION IV: DOWNSELL OFFERS

What to offer when they say no.

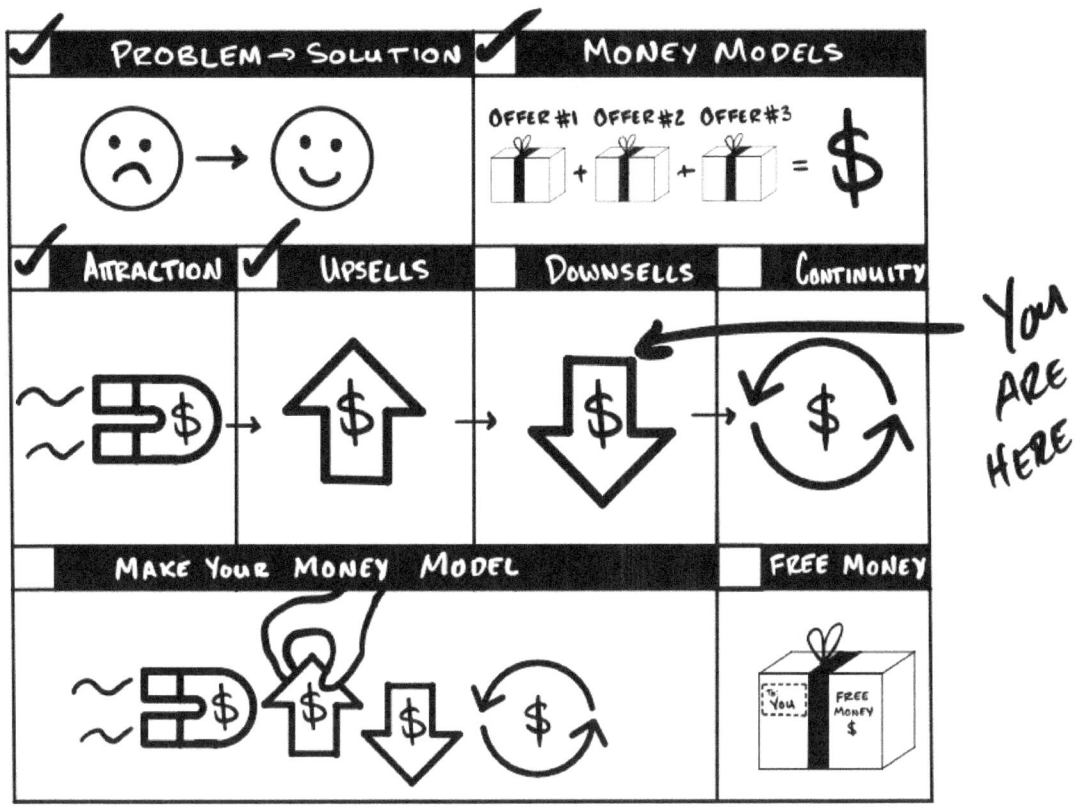

In the last section, we used Upsell Offers to get people to buy more stuff. If we did a good job, we've turned a profit too. Another step towards (or beyond!). Awesome… but what if they say no? → *We downsell them.*

Downselling tweaks the original offer to find the highest value solution *for the customer's budget*. So any offer you make after someone says "no" is a downsell.

I downsell in two ways. I change how they pay or *what they get*. For how they pay, I balance how much they pay now with how much they pay over time. For what they get, I change quantity, quality, or offer something different.

First, we cover my rules of downselling—*they apply to all my downsell processes*. Then, when we dive into individual offers, you can hit the ground running and downsell like a pro.

The Rules of Downselling

Remember, They Said No To *This* Offer, Not *All* Offers. Just because they rejected *this offer* does not mean they rejected *you*. It's an opportunity to find out what they really want. Stand your ground and make another offer. *No means no for this thing, not no for everything.*

Downsells Are Trades. When downselling, you work with the customer to find combinations of giving and getting until you get a match. <u>*If you're gonna give something, get something*</u>.

Personalize, Don't Pressure. Figure out what they like and don't like. Then, offer more of what they like and less of what they don't—*with a price to match*.

Offer The Same Things In New Ways. Limit downsells to what you've got. So just think of downselling more like a hundred ways to offer the stuff you already have, not 100 new products.

Don't Drop Your Price Just To Get Somebody To Buy. First off, dropping your price is not really downselling, *it's discounting*. On the other hand, you *can* offer them to pay less *now* and more money over time—a payment plan.

Next Up…

I use three simple and brutally effective downsell processes:

- Payment Plan Downsells *(how they pay)*
- Trial With Penalty *(how they pay)*
- Feature Downsells *(what they get)*

These downsell processes boost 30-day profit even further. They do it by making even more sales when customers would have said no. And I love them because with just a couple tweaks, you can fit them into your business and reap the rewards today.

Payment Plan Downsells

How much can you put down today?

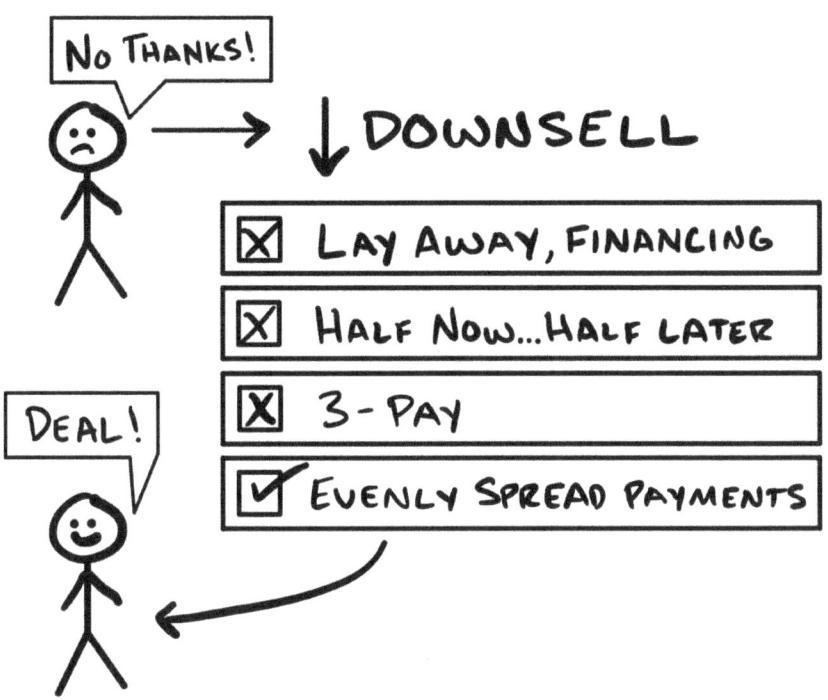

August 2013.

In my first month of business, with only one month's rent left in savings, I desperately needed to make sales to keep my gym afloat. When a potential customer said she couldn't afford my program, instead of giving up, I offered various payment options. Eventually, we agreed on a full payment on her payday, which was just before my rent was due. Two weeks later, I successfully charged her card, marking my first successful payment plan, and kept my business alive.

***

Payment plans are a gamble because they can make money in one way, *but they can lose money in two*. They make you more money when you get more customers and those customers complete their payments. They make you less money when people cancel before you turn a profit. You lose the most when people who would have paid in full take a payment plan—and cancel early.

This chapter maximizes how much money you make from payment plans and minimizes the money you lose.

Description

When most people think "downsell," they think of a lower amount, lower quality, cheaper, and so on. But I like to downsell by offering the same product again. Instead of offering a different thing, I spread the cost by charging some of it up front and putting the rest into scheduled payments. I call this a Payment Plan Downsell. Let's go over how they work.

Many people reject offers because they "cost too much." However, a *huge* percentage of the time "it costs too much" *really means* "this costs too much <u>up front</u>." So, Payment Plans get more buyers because customers pay less in the moment. But they also boost your profits because customers still pay full price over time.

My Payment Plan Downsell process takes up to seven steps. The process shifts from getting paid more up front to more over time. I stop when they buy. Here's my process.

Payment Plan Downsell Process Example

Step 1) Reward For Paying In Full Rather Than Punish For Paying Over Time. If I take on the risk of a payment plan, I increase the price. Normal businesses do it by charging interest, but everyone hates paying interest. So, I do it by offering a <u>discount</u> *if they pay in full*.

Step 2) Offer 3rd Party Financing, Credit Card, and Layaway Options

<u>3rd Party Financing</u>: This means another company pays me now and the customer has a payment plan *with that other company.*

<u>Credit Card</u>: Just ask "would you rather I decide your payment terms or you decide?" They say they'd prefer to decide. When they do, I tell them to use a credit card. That way I get paid today and they can pay the credit card company over time. I learned this reframe from a master salesman, and was surprised how well it works.

<u>Layaway</u>: Layaway means paying off the product *before* getting it. Customers can make as many installments as they want. They can take any reasonable amount of time to pay. But, they only get the product *after they've paid in full*. This is *by far* the most flexible for them and the lowest risk for us.

If they say no to these options, I move to step 3.

Step 3) Offer "Half Now, Half Later." I start by asking *"When's the next time you get paid?"* After, I ask *"Wanna just put half down today and the rest down when you get paid?"*

If they can't do that, I ask *"What's the most you can put down today?"* When they offer an amount say, *"Great. We'll put that down today and put the rest when you get paid. Fair enough?"* I like scheduling payments off of paychecks since most people get paid every two weeks. This boosts 30-day profit way more than monthly payments.

If they can't do those… I pause to make sure they actually want it.

Step 4) Check To See If They Still Want The Thing. I might say something like *"Got it. So money is tight right now. Real quick. I want to make sure. On a scale from 1–10 how bad do you wanna do this?"* If they say 8 or above, keep offering payment plans and say *"Awesome. Don't worry. We're gonna figure out a way to make this happen for you."* If they say 7 or below, ask *"Why not a 10?"* and then, say something like *"You're right. I think we may have something that could be a better fit for you."* Then you sell them something different (Feature Downsells—little later).

Step 5) Offer To Split Into Three Payments. If they said 8–10 on the scale, I downsell from half down to a third down. I offer a three-payment option: ⅓ now and ⅓ on the next two paychecks - *or* - ⅓ now and ⅓ next two months.

Step 6) Offer Evenly Spread Payments. If they still can't manage it, I evenly spread payments over the rest of their service. If that still creates problems, I move to step 7.

Step 7) Offer A Free Trial. I offer Free Trials in a special way. So, I dedicated the next chapter to it. But, the sale ends here. At least for now.

This Payment Plan Downsell process makes up to *nine* offers. And if you think that sounds crazy, you're probably making way less money and serving way fewer customers than you could.

Important Notes

Get Fewer Declined Payments. Align payment schedules with paycheck schedules. If you charge on days people get paid, they have a higher chance of paying.

How To Make Sure Payment Plans Make You Money. After implementing payment plans, your close rate should increase. But, if the number of paid-in-fulls goes down, you've just put people who would've paid in full on payment plans! So, *you want to close more appointments overall but with the same percentage of appointments paying in full.*

Exercise #16: Build Your Payment Plan Ladder

List the full price of your main offer. Then, write three payment plan options you could use.

Full Price: $ _____

Option 1 – Half Now, Half Later: _____

Option 2 – Three Payments: _____

Option 3 – Evenly Spread Plan (duration + amount): _____

Trial With Penalty

If you do X, Y, Z, I'll let you start for free.

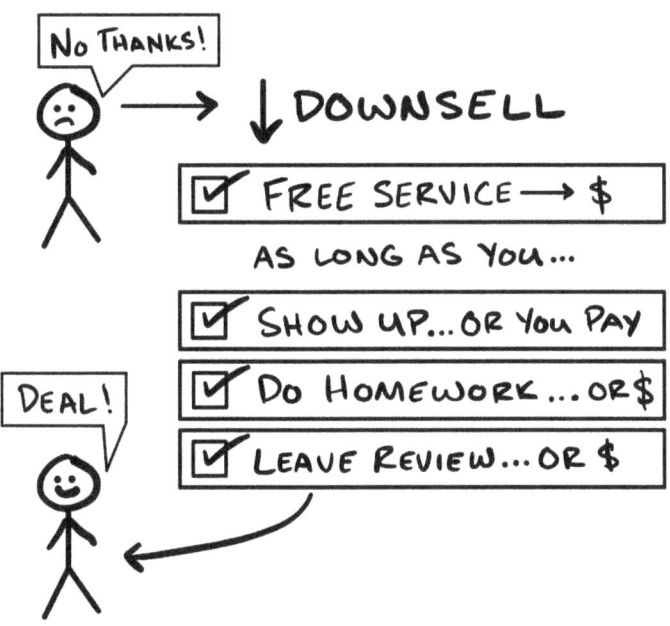

Spring 2018.

Gym Launch was growing fast. Leila needed better HR solutions and found a company with an interesting offer. The company offered free onboarding if Leila completed their training, but would charge for it *if she skipped the training*. This strategy forced Leila to learn their complex software. She ended up sticking with it because she didn't want to learn how to use another one.

Description

In a Trial With Penalty offer, customers can try your product or service for free *so long as they meet your terms*. Ideally, the terms should be things that make excellent customers. So, they'll mirror the actions and results used in your Win Your Money Back Offer. But this time, we use *avoiding fees* (rather than winning money back) to incentivize adherence.

To do a Trial With Penalty downsell, you must consider what they have to do to avoid the fee, and how you charge them. Normally, you get one chunk of people to buy your main offer. So, offer that first. And the rest, you'll get on this downsell.

If you only have one offer, you lose everyone who says no. Downselling trials with a penalty gives people another chance to say yes.

How To Downsell The Trial

Here's a graphic to show how I downsell a Trial with Penalty in five steps.

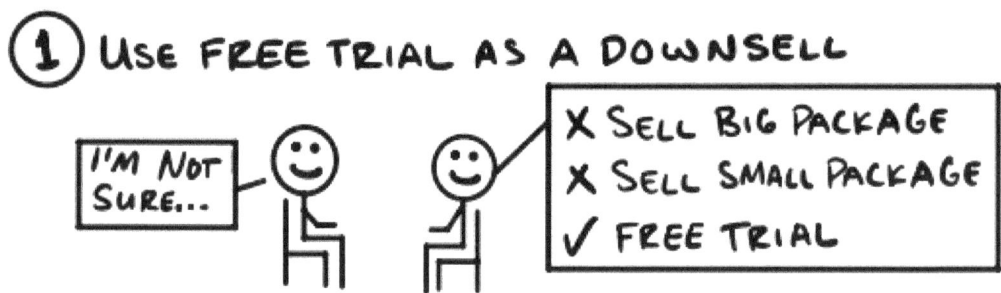

Offer The Trial Last. If someone makes it clear they don't want your first offer, then downsell the Trial With Penalty.

Always Get A Credit Card. Record their info, hold onto the ID, and motion for their credit card saying, *"What card you wanna use?"* They have to leave a card. If they balk, just say *"That's just how we've always done it."*

Always Sell Staying And Paying. Ask directly: *"If this program got you the result, would you stay long term?"* You want them to agree to staying long term if you get them results. If they say no, there's no point in giving them a trial. Once they agree, move on.

Explain the fees *after* getting their card. I say something like: *"We will do our part so long as you do yours. That's fair, right? So now I just ask that you bet on yourself - if you miss or skip any stuff, your results will suffer. We charge to keep you on track. If you miss, no big deal. You'll get dinged a little fee but it'll get you back on track. If you follow through, you get all this for free. So this is the best way we can get you amazing results and keep it free for you. Best of both worlds."*

Note: If you explain the fees *before* you get the card, you will get more resistance. So explain *after* with a *"this is just how we've always done it"* attitude.

Make Check-ins Required. First, we explain *all* criteria so they understand the costs and benefits of adhering. Then, we draw attention to check-ins (our upsell opportunities).

How I Upsell From A Trial. When someone takes a trial, one of three things happen: they like it, they hate it, or they don't use it. Here's how I upsell them from each scenario.

1) If they like it: This is the easy one. You already have them set up for automatic billing. Great! Meet with them anyway. You can still offer a longer term or higher value version of your service (or both). Successful customers tend to get even more value out of your better (and more profitable) stuff.

2) If they hate it: *Turn that frown upside down.* Ask them what they would have liked to be different. Tell them they're totally right, and that you're angry at yourself for missing this. *Do not blame them.* Only one person can be angry—and it needs to be you. Ask if they'll give you a chance to make it better because of how outraged you are at their experience. And now, since you better understand their needs, that they're a better fit for your higher level thing. Then, offer it to them. Yes—this is a sale. I can get about half of these people to buy.

3) If they didn't use it. *Reach out to people multiple times before you get to this point.* Explain that you need to meet with them. Offer to waive the fee if they do. Now, you can try to get them back on track or offer something better for them. I don't like billing non-starters. A small fee isn't worth a 1-star review. But hey, it's your choice.

What They Get For Free And What They Have To Do To Avoid The Fee. You'll need to know what your *terms of service* will be. The valuable parts will be either your bare bones offer (like the Decoy Offer) *or* your Win Your Money Back offer. Either work. I'd recommend giving more rather than giving less—if you can afford it. The criteria should activate and retain customers.

Breaking Up Fees vs. One Lump Fee. Say you have a $500 product with 10 things to do. I'd rather bill $50 for each mess up than one $500 fee on their first mess up. On the other hand, if missing once really messes up their success, you'll want the fee to reflect that. I've seen both work.

Let People Make Up For Goofs. People often get discouraged after getting billed. But, you can offer an opportunity to "make it up." This does a great job of getting people back on track and converting. But, if they miss that, you're justified in billing them.

Pay Less Now or Pay More Later vs. Trial With Penalty. I use Pay Less Now or Pay More Later as a downsell for physical products or one-time services. And I use Trial With Penalty as a downsell for recurring products or services.

Exercise #17: Create Your Free Trial With Penalty

1. Write down the total Price/Penalty if they don't do what they're supposed to: $ _____

2. Write down the terms of your trial:

    a. Action they must take #1: _____

       i. Price/Penalty if they don't: $ _____

    b. Action they must take #2: _____

       i. Price/Penalty if they don't: $ _____

    c. Action they must take #3: _____

       i. Price/Penalty if they don't: $ _____

    d. Meeting they must attend #1: _____

       i. Price/Penalty if they don't: $ _____

    e. Meeting they must attend #2: _____

       i. Price/Penalty if they don't: $ _____

    f. Meeting they must attend #3: _____

       i. Price/Penalty if they don't: $ _____

> **FREE GIFT: Free Trial Training**
>
> Not all businesses can do free trials. But if you can, it's a helluva downsell. There's obviously right and wrong ways to do them and right and wrong businesses to do them in. I made a free video for you covering this chapter and as many details as I could. You can watch it at acquisition.com/training/money. I put a QR code for fast easy access.
>
>

Feature Downsells

Why don't we try this instead?

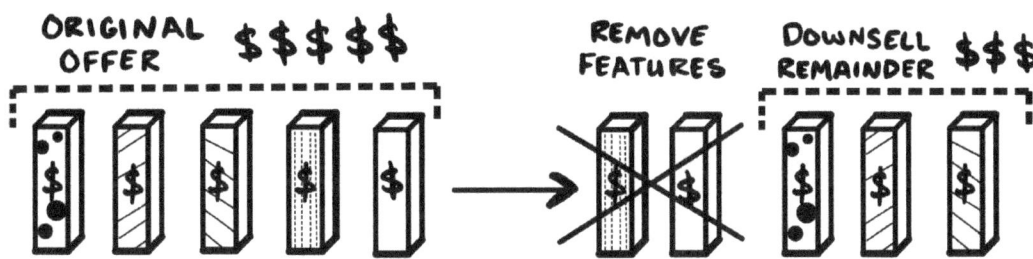

I can't remember when in 2019.

A business owner friend showed me a new downsell that tripled his close rate from 25% to 75%, without using payment plans or traditional discounts. He offered a lower price by removing the money-back guarantee he typically offered. So, he treated it like a feature he could add or remove with a value associated with it. This downsell increased his overall sales but also boosted paid-in-fulls. The moment customers realized they'd lose the guarantee, they realized they wanted it even more.

The results were significant: out of 100 potential customers, 35 now buy the main product (up from 25), and an additional 40 take the downsell (zero guarantee) option.

Description

Feature Downsells lower prices by changing what customers get. I do them by offering less quantity, lower quality, lower price alternatives, or cutting optional components.

All features have a price and a value. If you remove something the price goes down, sure. But, the value goes down too. What features you remove and how much you lower the price affects how good of a deal the person gets. This change in your offer's price-to-value affects how people buy. People wanna get the *best deal for them.*

For instance, if you remove stuff they hate, and lower the price a lot, they get a *better deal.* If you remove stuff they love, and lower the price a little, they get a *worse deal.* Both get people to buy. In the story, customers loved the guarantee. *The guarantee had far more value than its price.* So even if they said no at first, removing the guarantee instantly showed its value. The customers saw the higher-price offer as *a better deal.* So, after seeing the downsell option, they bought the first offer.

People will see the value in the thing you removed *after they see the difference in price*. As in, people weigh how much money they save against how much value they lose. So, clever Feature Downselling gets customers to "re-upsell" themselves on the more expensive offers. This means you want to r*emove features from highest to lowest value*. Since people want more value for their money, this incentivizes customers to make the <u>highest value</u> purchase for them.

Feature Downsells have a simple formula: Take something away, lower the price, and in so many words ask "How about now?"

Feature Downsell Examples

Feature Downselling <u>Product Quality</u>. Think older versions, less reliable materials, materials of lower social status, etc.

<u>Product Quality Downsell</u>: *Instead of the leather seats we can do vinyl, how does that sound?*

Feature Downselling <u>Service Quality</u>. This means a lot of things. I will give you a few ways I change the quality of services. Hint: This also works to *increase* the service quality.

<u>Service Quality Downsell</u>: *Instead of 5-minute response times, why don't we just start you at overnight response times? You'll save some money and you'll still get your answers - just with a small delay.*

<u>More Service Quality Features</u>:
- <u>Time Availability</u>: Come specific times vs. whenever you want
    - Days of the week: Mon/Wed/Fri vs. All Days
    - Times of day: 9 to 5 vs. 24hrs
    - Amount of time: 15min Support Calls vs. 60min Support Calls
- <u>Location Availability</u>: This one location vs. all locations we own
- <u>Cancellations</u>: Reschedule fees vs. free
- <u>Speed Of Response</u>: Reply in minutes vs. hours vs. days etc.
- <u>Speed Of Delivery</u>: Wait in line vs. priority, same day/next day vs. next week, etc.
- <u>Service Ratio</u>: One-on-one vs. one-to-many vs. many-to-one

- Communication Method: Text support vs. chat support vs. video call support, etc.
- Provider Qualifications: Owner vs. long-time employee vs. new employee, etc.
- Live vs. Recorded: Watch it happening now vs. watch it *after* it happens later
- In-Person vs. Remote: Watch where it happens vs. watch it somewhere else
- DIY, DWY, DFY. Do It Yourself vs. Done With You vs. Done For You
- Expirations: Works forever vs. works for X time vs. works at specific times
- Personalization: Generic vs. made just for you
- Insurance/Guarantee:
    - Lengths of time: For One Year vs. For Life
    - Coverage: Specific bad thing happens vs. Any bad thing happens
    - Terms: Unconditional vs. Only if you do XYZ

Downselling by Removing Entire Features. Rather than lowering quantity or quality, you remove the feature itself. In the story above, he removed a guarantee.

Removing Entire Feature Downsell: *Instead of priority chat support, email support, and calls, why don't we just keep chat and email support but drop the calls to save you some money? You'll still get your answers, it'll just save us time and we can pass those savings to you.*

Feature Downselling Done-For-You to Do-It-Yourself. If someone says no to all your service downsells, you can downsell another product that solves the same problem.

Done-For-You to Do-It-Yourself Product Downsell:

- Chiropractor: *Instead of chiropractic adjustments, let's start you with some tools you can use to do it yourself at home?* Then, you'd sell at-home massage tools, foam rollers, mats, etc.
- Painter: *If you can't afford me painting your house, why don't I just give you the paint and let you lease one of our spray machines for a daily rate?*
- Alex Hormozi: *Instead of me and my team buying your company and actively growing your business, why don't you just attend a workshop?* (*Cough* Go to acquisition.com)

Important Notes

Remember, Never Negotiate The Price. Don't let anyone pay less *just because*.

Maintain The Position Of A Helpful Guide. Remember, Feature Downselling means trying to find *the best deal for them*.

Tweak Your Feature Downsell Process. We have the job of making the product have the highest value-to-cost *in the eyes of the customer*. But, in the beginning, you won't know much about your customers' preferences. So, as you solve the same problems for the same type of customer, you'll learn what they find the most valuable.

How I Standardize My Downsell Process. First, I cut something valuable and lower the price *a little*. I do this to get them to reconsider the original offer/price. If that fails, I continue removing features and lowering prices until they buy. I'd rather people get *something* rather than nothing.

Name Your Feature Combinations. Name the most expensive combination after a status your customer would find aspirational: "The Whale Package" "The Total Transformation" "High Roller" etc. Look at airlines. Make your version of First Class→Business Class→Economy.

I Name My Cheapest Combination "The Minimum." I like it because it implies they have to get *at least* that thing. If someone rejects all other packages, I just say "So nothing more than the minimum package then?" To get them to say no to say yes (like the Classic Upsell).

After Each Downsell, Ask "Deal?" Or "Fair Enough?" This works *astonishingly* well. Fewer people will see you change the offer for them and then say "No that's not fair." Listen to how I present Feature Downsells in Episode 202 of my podcast The Game, "How to close everyone downselling like a pro."

Free Orientations Boost Do-It-Yourself Feature Downsells. Once someone has refused all my Done For You offers, I ask *"Even though we're not gonna work together on X, I still want to help. How about you just come to a free orientation on X tomorrow?"* At the end of the orientation, I offer a DIY product that solves the same problem as the DFY service.

Feature Downsell Your Guarantees. If you already have a guarantee, make removing it part of your Feature Downsell process. People value security, so removing it makes many realize its value. This often flips an initial "no" back to a "yes."

Feature Downsell Current Customers. Customers who use all the features they pay for keep paying longer than people who don't. So once you see a customer isn't using a feature, offer a lower price—only paying for the features they use. They'll either tell you they want to keep it and might start using it again—or—they'll be happy you gave them a *better deal*.

Barter With Reviews, Testimonials, And Referrals. Bartering is the oldest form of exchange. If I get a price objection, sometimes I offer discounts in exchange for advertising. Ex: *"I'll knock $100 off if you: 1) Leave me a review on all review sites 2) Leave me a video testimonial 3) Make a public social post at the beginning, middle, and end of our program showing your progress 4) Introduce me to two friends who you would want to do this with. Deal?"* To me, the advertising is worth more than the $100 discount. To them, the $100 is worth less than the advertising. Win-win.

Exercise #18: Build Your Feature Downsells

1. Feature Downsell #1 (Valuable thing they want): _____
   a. Discount Applied (small): $ _____
2. Feature Downsell #2 (Thing they want *less*): _____
   a. Discount Applied (medium): $ _____
3. Feature Downsell #3 (Thing they want *less*): _____
   a. Discount Applied (medium): $ _____
4. Feature Downsell #4 (Thing they want *less*): _____
   a. Discount Applied (large): $ _____

FREE GIFT: Feature Downsell Training [No Opt-in]

Understanding features within services and products gives you a huge advantage. It can help you make your stuff super profitable *while* staying attractive to the customer. This is one of my favorite topics and I made you an additional training that covers it. You can watch it, as always, at acquisition.com/training/money. I put a QR code for fast easy access.

Downsell Offers Conclusion

Everybody buys something.

Downsells give you another shot at getting a customer by turning *nos* into *yeses*. For that reason, it's less about having a hundred different products with the same offer, and more about having a hundred different offers for the same product. But, no matter what, the offer is *never the same stuff for cheaper*. We just keep tweaking the offer until we make it *the best deal for them*. The extra cash explodes our 30-day profits and blows us past our goals.

So we've used attraction offers to get customers to *buy once*. We've used upsells to get them to buy the next thing. And now I've shown you my three most powerful downsell processes *in case they say no*: Payment Plan Downsells, Trial With Penalty, and Feature Downsells.

Next, we've got the final stage of a *$100M Money Model*—Continuity Offers: *how to keep them buying for good*.

Exercise #19: Pick Your Downsell Offer

Pick the downsell offers you will start using to get more people to say yes. Refer to your exercise answers from this section and start using your downsells. Check all that you plan on using:

a. Payment Plan Downsells ( )

b. Trial With Penalty ( )

c. Feature Downsells ( )

SECTION V: CONTINUITY OFFERS

You can shear a sheep for a lifetime, but you can only skin it once. - John, an early mentor

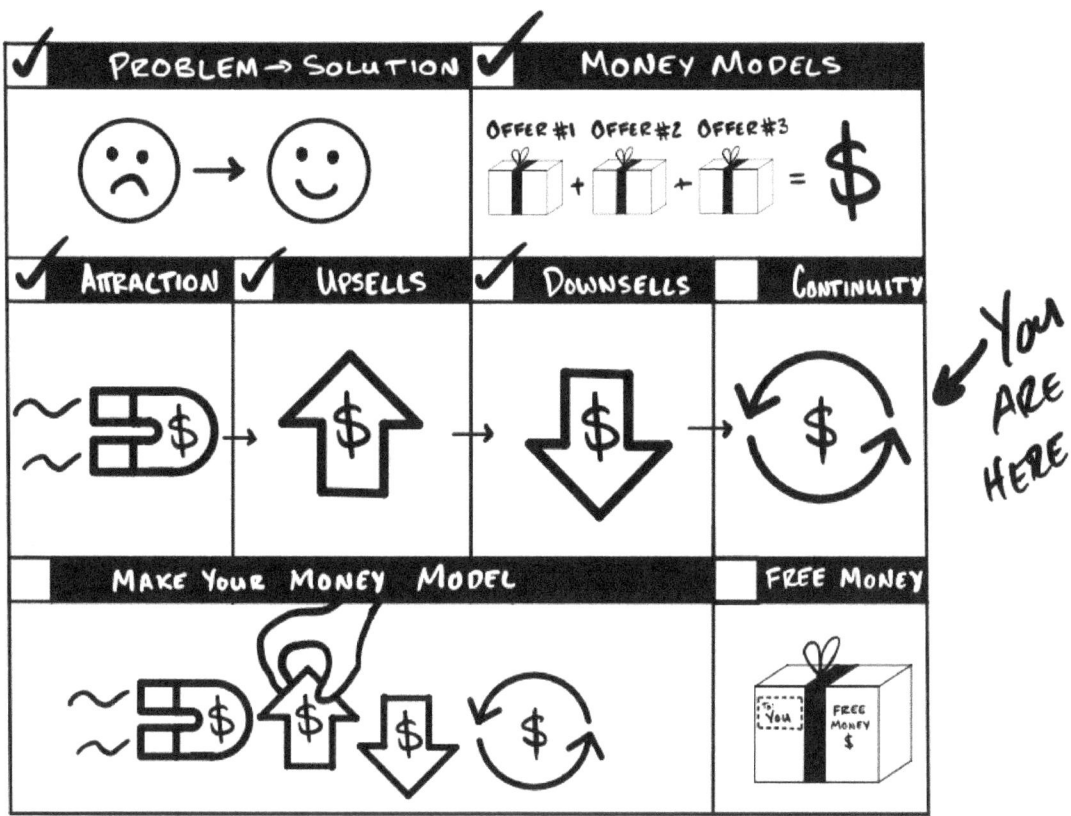

When you do continuity right, you get more customers *and* make more money from them. Continuity Offers *provide ongoing value that customers make ongoing payments for—until they cancel.* They boost the profit from every customer and give you one last thing to sell. Continuity Offers are awesome because you sell once, but get paid again and again.

Let me explain.

Let's say you offer a $1,000 thing to 100 people and 10 buy—you make $10,000 (10 x $1,000).

Now, let's say you talk to the same 100 people but you make your $1,000 thing… $50 per month instead. At 50 bucks, we can get 40 out of 100 to buy. And, if you keep those people for twenty months, *you still make $1,000 from each customer.* You go from making $10,000 now and $0 over time to $2,000 now and $40,000 over time.

As an added bonus, in the first example, if you only sold 10 customers, you'd only have 10 customers to upsell later. If you used a Continuity Offer and sold 40 customers, you'd have four times the customers to upsell later. A massive difference.

This illustrates the pros and cons of continuity. You can attract more customers compared to something more expensive, but you make *way* less money *now*. That makes it tough to use as an Attraction Offer *on its own*. Even if you have more money-making potential tomorrow, Continuity Attraction Offers leave you strapped for cash today.

By making continuity offers *last*, we get the best of all worlds. We get cash today from Attraction Offers, Upsell Offers, and Downsell Offers. We get a little cash today and tons of cash tomorrow from Continuity Offers.

To be clear—you can make Continuity Offers wherever and however you want. They can attract new customers, upsell and downsell current customers, or re-engage old customers.

Also, only *some* stuff makes sense for a continuity offer. It's silly for someone to pay for a one-day workshop… forever. It makes sense for them to pay until they cover the cost—and that makes it a payment plan. At the same time, you probably make a mistake to offer a single price (even a big price) to provide a service forever. If your customers get ongoing value, it probably makes sense for them to make ongoing payments.

The Three Continuity Offers

All offers depend on getting customers to buy. But, Continuity Offers depend on getting customers to keep buying. I get them to do both by combining bonuses, discounts, and fees.

- Continuity: Bonus Offers
- Continuity: Discount Offers
- Waived Fee Offer

Now that we got that covered. You can't get customers to stick to your continuity offer unless they've started… so let's start there.

Continuity Bonus Offers

If you like this, you're gonna love what I have next…

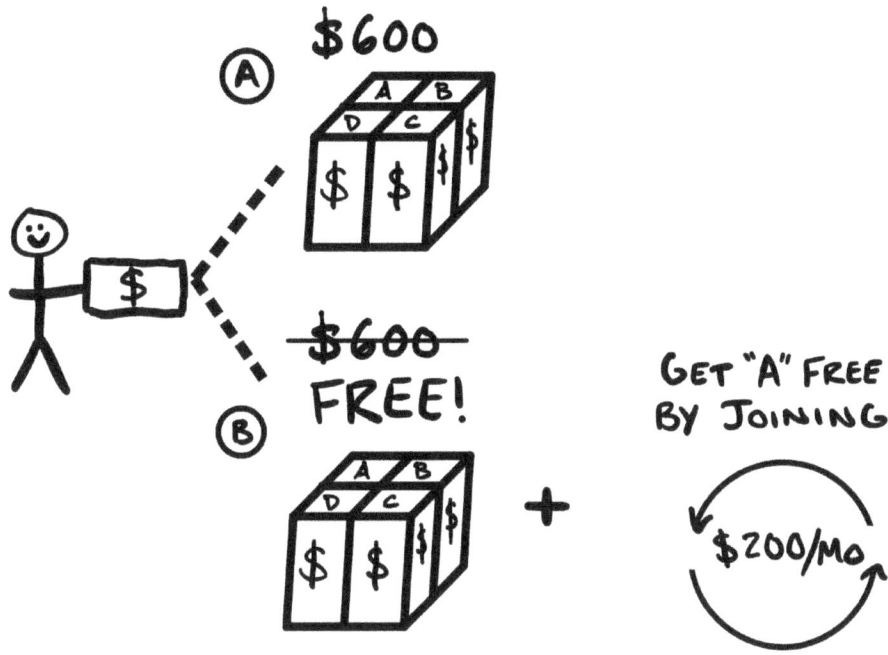

Fall 2019. When I learned that bonuses got more people to join continuity programs…

A gym owner came to me boasting huge numbers. He had tweaked my standard six-week challenge "Win Your Money Back" offer. Instead of selling it directly, he offered it as a standalone offer and separately as a free gift with a membership. The tweak *tripled* his membership sales while maintaining up front cash payments because some people still bought the standalone offer.

Later, he figured out a way to get even more cash by upselling a discounted six-month prepaid membership to new members within the first few weeks. This clever tweak transformed his gym and became a staple in my money models.

Description

With Continuity Bonuses you give the customer an awesome thing *if* they sign up today. Typically, the bonus itself has more value than the first continuity payment. That's all there is to it.

Bonus—adding value. For products, you can give away many small things or one big product that complements the subscription. For services, you give away a defined program, onboarding, setup, or a feature that adds value.

Discount—lowering costs. Remember, anything you offer for free you can also offer as a discount. Free stuff and discounts both affect how we make decisions. So, we want to do *both* to get the benefits of both.

When making continuity offers, I get more people to *start* if I add more good stuff (bonuses) and take away bad stuff (discounts). And of course, it all works better with a dash of urgency—if they join *now*. Also, you can offer the bonus as a standalone purchase, or you can *only* make it available if they buy your continuity. Either works.

On their own, continuity offers get less cash now, and that makes it tough for getting customers profitably. But the way I use them, we can still hit our 30-day profit goals. Here's how: First, I do all my big-cash Attraction, Upsell, and Downsell offers. Then, Continuity Offers get a little bit of cash from the first month's payments. Then, I offer people who bought one month a discount on prepaying more months. This further boosts 30-day profits, giving me more cash to advertise, *and* stacks recurring revenue. Not too shabby.

Examples Of Getting People To Start On Continuity

Physical Product: Pet Food Continuity Offer

One-Time Bonus: Get every dog toy we've ever made for free, an $800 value, when you sign up for monthly dog food shipments for $59 per month.

Monthly Bonuses: You'll get a new dog toy every month as a member.

Service: Short-Term Accelerator Offer

One-Time Bonus: Short-Term Accelerator costs $1,000 on its own. Get it free when you become a member for $100 per month.

Bonus Package: The VIP community members enjoy first in line access to our events, longer support hours, better support reps, etc.

Digital Product Offer

One-Time Bonus: Get all my past 40 newsletters valued at $15,880 by becoming a member today for only $399/mo after a 30-day free trial.

Lifetime Discount + Lifetime Bonuses: If you pay today, you can lock in a lifetime discount to $299 per month. Get early digital access *and* a physical copy every month.

Note: Use the elements from the Feature Downsell chapter to create better bonuses.

Important Notes

Focus On The Bonus, Not The Membership. "Join my membership program" isn't nearly as compelling as "get this free valuable thing." So advertise that. Then, explain the rest after they show interest.

Bonuses Work Kinda Like Upsells.

More of the same: You get two years of past newsletters free by becoming a member.

Complementary: You get nutrition services for free when you sign up for our fitness membership.

Upgrade: You get a free gold membership when you buy a bronze membership (limited availability).

Keep Your Bonuses Related To Your Core Offer. If the bonus is too different you will *attract the wrong customers.* For instance, don't advertise a free t-shirt to upsell tech services. But, advertising a free t-shirt to upsell t-shirt printing makes sense.

Make Bonuses Things You Already Have And Do. For instance, the two past years of newsletters cost no extra time but are super high value. And onboarding is something you have to do with the client anyways, so you might as well slap a price on it and give it to 'em as a bonus. If you value it, they will too.

Physical Bonuses on Digital Products and Digital Bonuses with Physical Products. If I have a digital membership, I might offer a hat, shirt, or tool, etc. related to the offer. If I have a physical product or service, like a boxing gym membership, offering live stream classes can get more people to sign up. This strategy often lowers the cost of getting a customer more than the cost of the bonus.

You Can Make Free Bonuses Discounts and Make Discounts Free Bonuses.

Free Bonus: Become a member for $200 then you get this $1,000 program as a free bonus!

Steep Discount: Get the $1,000 program for $1 if you become a member for $200.

When Making Your Continuity Offer, Anchor The Bonuses. First, sell them the benefits of the amazing bonus. Not your continuity offer—the bonus. Then, use your high-value bonus as an anchor. It may shock them—and *that's okay*. Because then you ask, "Do you want to know how you can get this for free?" If they do, which they will, explain how: *"Become a VIP member today and you'll get it all as a free gift for joining. Or, you can just buy it for $XXX—which would you prefer?"*

More Bonuses Get More People To Join. After you ask them if they want to know how to get it for free, you tell them they can get it when they join. Then you say *"On top of that…* when you become a member you'll get… amazing thing 1, amazing thing 2, amazing thing 3." *Mention the individual dollar values of each to anchor the value.* Stacking bonuses this way gets even more people to join your continuity.

Making Bonuses Available Only To Those Who Join. If you want to force everyone into continuity, then offer continuity as the only option. In other words, make the bonuses *only available* if they join the membership.

Pricing For Continuity vs. Up front Cash. For whatever reason, some people pick one-time payments over continuity… *even with higher one-time payments.* So offer a higher one-time payment option. This way some customers will make you more money *today* while others stack recurring revenue for *tomorrow. The smaller the standalone price compared to the continuity price, the more people buy the standalone. The larger the standalone price compared to the continuity price, the more people choose continuity.*

If You Want Even More Cash—Offer Bulk Prepaid Discounts. Bulk continuity upsells boost 30-day profits by a lot. Let's say you offer "buy five months get one free." Only *one out of every eight people* has to take the upsell to raise 30-day profits by 50%!

If You Want Commitments. You can pair the bonus with a commitment. For example, only allow customers to get the bonus if they join and commit to 3-6-12+ months. You will get more people to commit this way, but fewer will take it—at least compared to giving it to everyone. In the beginning, keep it simple. Just offer bonuses standalone and continuity month-to-month.

Exercise #20: Create Your Continuity Bonus

1. Write out your "one-time program" price (that you'll give as a free <u>bonus</u>):

    $ _____

    a. Bonus Component #1 *(more)*: _____

    b. Bonus Component #2 *(better)*: _____

    c. Bonus Component #3 *(different)*: _____

    d. Bonus Component #4: _____

    e. Guarantee: _____

2. Write out your continuity price (should be ⅓ to ⅕ the price of bonus):

    $ _____

    a. Exclusive Member Bonus #1: _____

    b. Exclusive Member Bonus #2: _____

    c. Exclusive Member Bonus #3: _____

3. Write out your prepaid annual continuity price: (10x monthly from above):

    $ _____

    a. One big bonus they get for prepaying: _____

Continuity Discount Offers

If you sign up today, you get X time free.

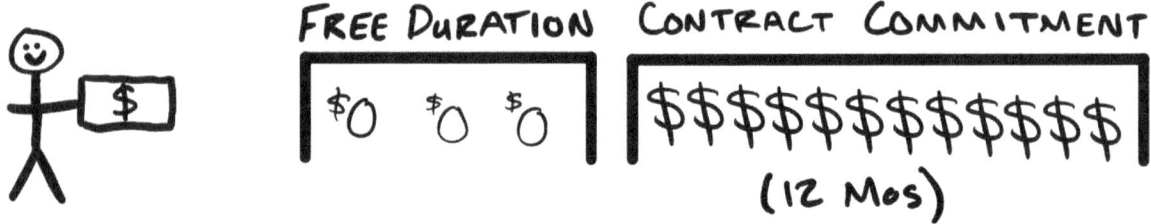

Spring 2018.

While settling into a new neighborhood, I met a neighbor who turned out to be a successful businessman in an unexpected industry: trash. He told me the secret to his success: offering a year of free service to large apartments in exchange for five-year paid contracts. The offer won over big customers from competitors, and got his customers for cheap. Despite losing money the first year because of all the free labor he fronted, his gamble paid off. He ended up scaling and selling the business for millions.

Description

To make a one-time continuity discount, you give products or services away for free if the customer commits to buying more products and services *over time*. This can attract loads of potential customers and makes an easy sale anyone can close.

If you look around, you'll see this offer in many different industries. It works. Think internet, pool cleaning, gym memberships, landscaping, and anything rentable.

You can make this work in any business so long as you know two things. First, how you'll apply the discount—I do it four ways. And second, your cancellation policy—because people don't always keep their commitments.

I discount in <u>four</u> ways: Up front, at the end, an even spread, or after the first month or two.

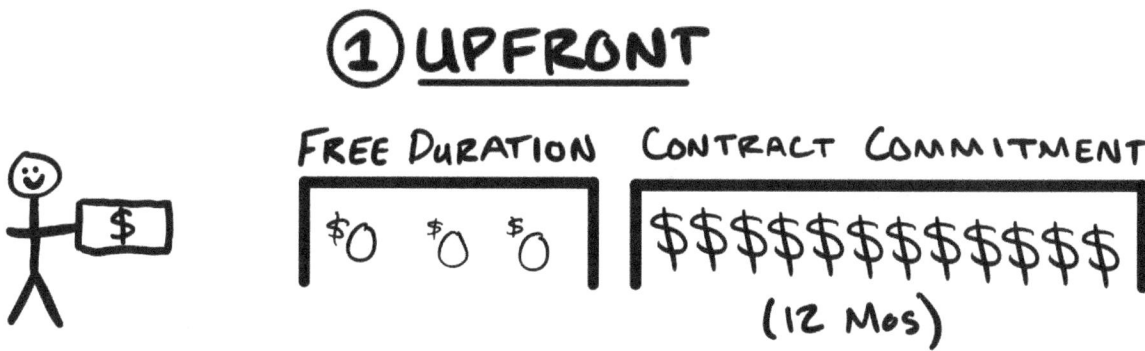

Up Front. You apply the discount up front and push out the term. As in, the "official" time starts after their free time ends. This works best in industries that have a successful history of enforcing contracts (cell phones, storage, real estate, equipment, or anything with collateral). Two notes: First, if you have historically high churn, then skip this one and consider the others. Second, this does not get customers profitably. It gets customers, but delays cash. So if you want more profitable options, continue on.

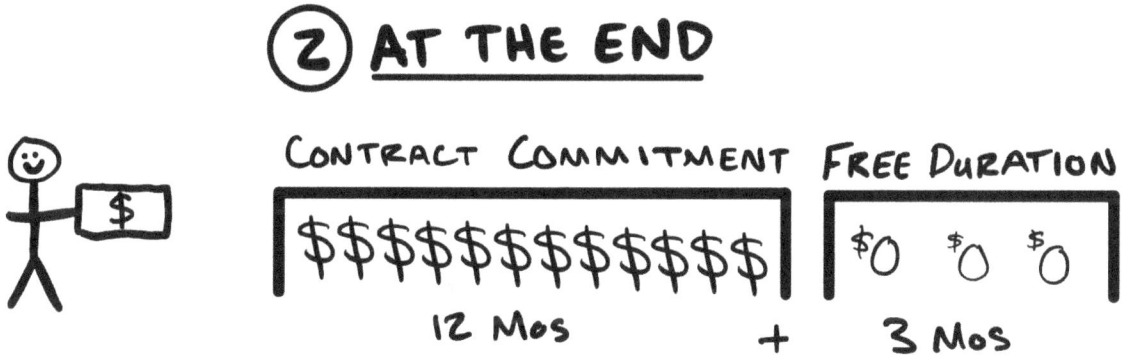

At The End. You can apply the entire discount at the end and push out the term. So long as they make every payment *on time*… they get a bonus time equal to the value of the discount. They *earn* their free time.

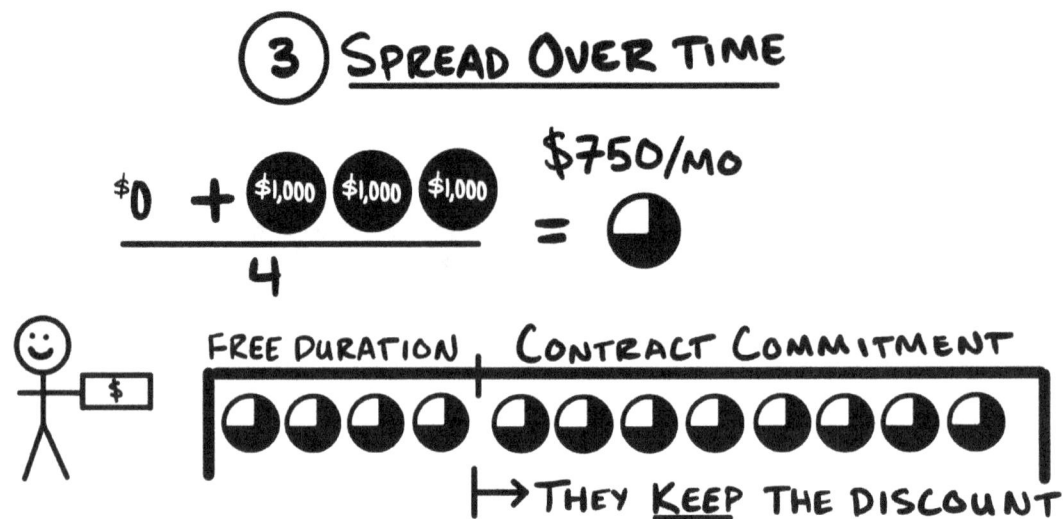

Spread Over Time. Apply the discount across the term. Say you give three months free for a one-year commitment. At $200 per month you've discounted $600. By spreading that $600 over 12 months, they get a $600/12 months = $50 discount *each month*. You can also tell them that if they make all their payments on time, they can keep the discount for life after the term is over.

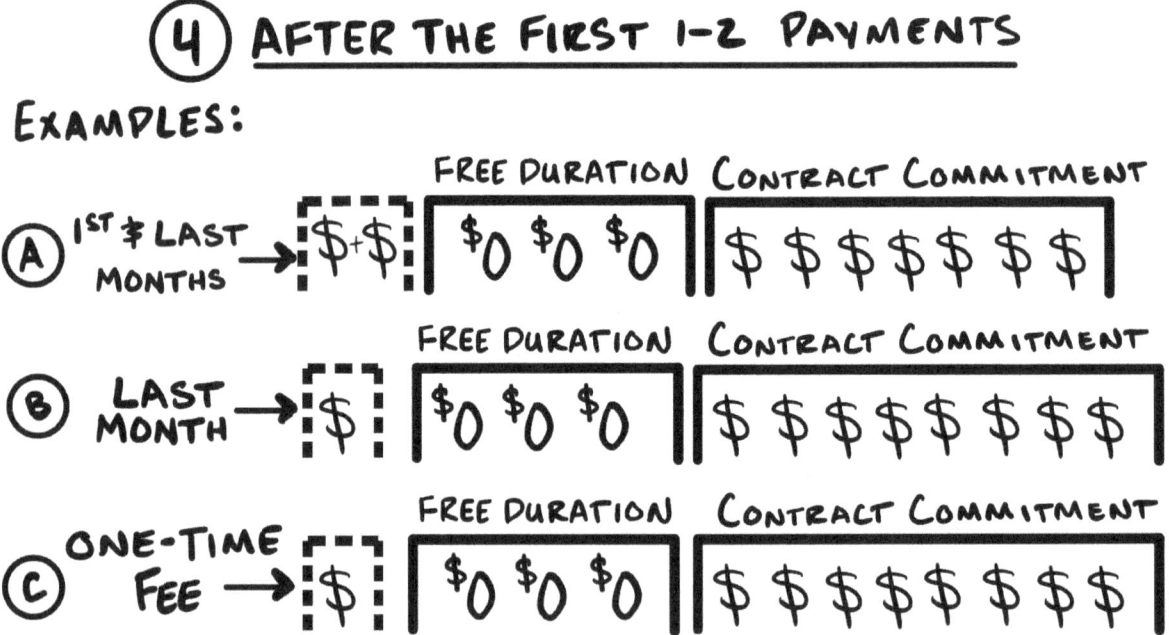

After the first one or two payments. They pay a few times and then they get their one-time discount. This way you collect a bit of cash to cover advertising and some delivery costs. I prefer to do it by presenting the offer as *"first and last month," "last month up front,"* or adding some sort of *activation fee* before getting the bonus value. It also ensures the customer uses a valid form of payment… a small but important detail when you run a business.

CANCELLATIONS

You Need To Have A Cancellation Policy Figured Out Ahead Of Time. There are many common ones. 30 or 60 days notice. Cancellation fees. Cancel anytime. Etc. Since everyone comes into my Continuity Offers on a discount of some kind, this is my favorite:

Just make the cancellation fee *equal to the discount they agreed to get.* So if they got $600 in discounts by committing, they can pay $600 whenever they want to cancel. This is simple to explain.

Make Sure Customers Know How To Cancel. Have a clear way for them to contact you, then you can have a real chance to save it.

If A Customer Wants To Cancel, Ask To Do An Exit Interview. I might say "I'll waive your cancellation fee if you come in and tell me what I could do better." This gives customers a *real* reason to give feedback. Then, I can use their feedback to fix the problem—or—offer something better suited for them. At the very least, they'll have nicer things to say about the business if I actually try to solve the problem. I routinely save a third of customers who agree to exit interviews.

Important Notes

Highest Value Per Word Note In This Book Skip this if you hate money. Bill on *week-increments, not month-increments.* (every 4 weeks, 12 weeks etc). Here's why. There are 12 months in a year, but the year has 13 four-week cycles. *That's an 8.3% difference.*

Don't Eat Into The Term With Discounts, Extend Them! Let's say you offer three months free when you sign up for a year. That could mean they pay for nine months then get three free (12 total months). Or, that could mean they pay twelve months and get three free (15 total months). I prefer to start with extending the term. Then, I can Feature Downsell a shorter one.

Get 3% More Revenue For Four Extra Words. "Yeah, it's $X *plus a 3% processing fee.*" In my life, I've never had anyone not buy because of a processing fee. But 3% added to your topline *for no extra work* goes straight to your bottom line. If you run a 10% profit business, and add 3%, you just added 30% to your profit. Worth it. And this works especially well when paired with…

Get Two Forms Of Payment. Recurring businesses lose mountains of cash because of payment processing problems. First, customers don't cancel but their payment information changes or expires. Second, customers max out cards or have insufficient funds. We fix both issues with the same solution. I ask them if they want to save the 3% processing fee by giving us a second form of payment.

Try Lifetime Discount At Your Most Common Churn Point. You advertise the lifetime discount. But, you make customers *earn* it. They get a lower rate *if* they stay past X period. Make X the month your average customer drops off.

Real-world example: I saw a rice company selling (a lot) of rice. They offered three pricing options: 1) a one-time price 2) a 5% off subscription and 3) 15% off *if you stayed on the subscription for five straight months.* You earned the lifetime lower rate. I'm sure they figured out that it was just beyond where most people canceled.

Exercise #21: Create Your Continuity Discount Offer

1. What amount of time or product you want to give away free: _____

2. Pick when you want to give it (Circle One):

    a. Up front

    b. Over time

    c. At the end

    d. After the first few payments

3. Pick term length: _____

    a. Script it: *"If you commit to [term length] months, you'll get [free time/discount structure]. That's a total value of $ _____ for just $ _____ per month. Want me to lock that in for you?"*

4. Pick if/when you want to give a lifetime discount (after your churn point): _____

5. Create cancellation terms:

    a. Add exit interview to terms (Y / N) + Add incentive to take interview _____

    b. Add cancellation fee equal to time given if they break the agreement (Y / N)

c. Script it: *"To honor the discount, we ask for [X days'] notice or the option to pay the difference if canceled early. That way, everything stays fair. Sound good?"*

FREE GIFT: Continuity Discount Offers Training

Like bonuses, discounts are only limited by your creativity. In this chapter I gave you the building blocks. I also made you a video covering some of the creative ways I've seen. As usual, you can watch it free at acquisition.com/training/money. Or, scan the QR code. Enjoy.

Waived Fee Offer

You can sign up month to month with a setup fee, or I'll waive it if you commit to a year.

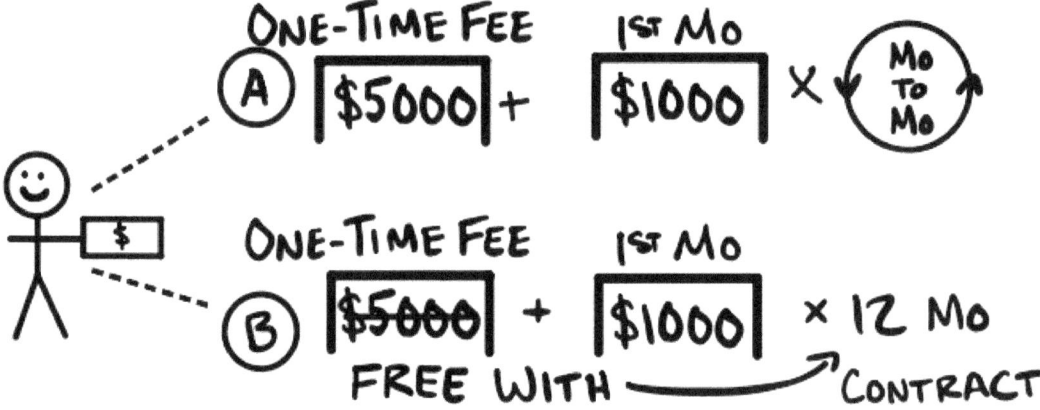

January 2021.

I met a high-ticket salesman with higher close rates and lower churn than I did. So, I asked him how he did it. Here's how: he offered customers two options: a month-to-month plan with a large setup fee, or a year-long commitment with the fee waived. The waived large setup fee got customers to commit to the year-long plan to get the savings, while also making early cancellation more painful. It was the holy grail, with higher conversion rates and higher LTV.

Description

Waived Fee Offers work like this. First, you ask the customer to pay a startup fee as part of joining a month-to-month program. Typically, I do 3–5x my monthly rate. Then, you offer to discount the *entire* fee *if* they commit longer term. But, if they cancel inside the term, they pay the fee.

Customers can choose to pay a significant fee and keep the option to quit at any time, or they can commit to 12 months and get the fee waived. Many will commit to avoid the big fee.

We take a greater risk if they pay month-to-month. But *they* take a greater risk if they commit. If a customer chooses month-to-month, we lower our risk with the startup fee. But, we lower *their* risk year-to-year by waiving those fees. And if they commit and want to quit early, then OK. They pay *as if* they had chosen "month-to-month" from the beginning. Simple.

Bottom Line: Customers will stay longer if leaving costs more than staying.

Example

Since the offer focuses more on pricing, it looks the same in all continuity businesses. The following example pulls from the story to give you a closer look at the mechanics.

Waived Fees With Commitment.

1) Commitment length - 12 months

2) Monthly rate - $1,000 per month

3) Fee - $5,000 *if they pay month-to-month.*

Option A: Pay a one-time fee of $5,000 *plus* $1,000 for the first month. Then pay $1,000 per month thereafter. Cancel whenever you want.

Option B: Waive the $5,000 if you commit to 12 months. Pay $1,000 per month. Only pay the $5,000 fee if you break your commitment early.

Important Notes

Fees Get Them To Start. People get value out of committing *immediately* because they avoid a fee. People want to avoid fees. So, more people sign up to continuity.

Fees Get Them To Stick. People will stick for the same reason they started. By sticking, *they avoid the fee.* People quit for millions of reasons. But, by incurring an additional and larger fee *in order to* cancel, their original reason for quitting immediately shrinks compared to the value of avoiding the fee. In English, if the cost to quit exceeds the cost to stay, they will probably stay.

Presenting The Fee. Justify the fee by explaining the costs of taking on new customers for long-term programs. Basically, if they want short-term flexibility, *they pay their own setup costs.* But, if they commit to staying long-term, *we pay their setup costs for them.* If someone asks for additional reasoning, just say: *"It costs us money to get you started. If you only wanna test us out, you cover those costs. If you commit longer, I'll cover them."*

If More Than 5% Of People Want To Cancel Early, Look Into It. Pricing *incentivizes* sticking but it can't (and *shouldn't*) overcome a terrible product.

If You Want More Up Front Cash, Have A Smaller Fee. A smaller fee encourages people to go month-to-month. A larger fee encourages people to make the commitment. But if you need more cash up front, you can make the fee 1.5–3x the monthly rate. When you do this, more people will take it, and you'll get more cash up front.

Drop The Fee After The Customer Fulfills The Commitment. If someone stays the entirety of their commitment, then wants to cancel, they have earned their free cancellation.

I Prefer This Offer For Commitments Of One Year And Longer. The longer the commitment, the better this works. It works especially well with services that take a long time to work (SEO, Investing, Weight Loss, etc). It keeps people committed when they get emotional.

Cancellation Fees For A… Cause? If you want to keep customers extra motivated—you can donate it to a cause they are *against*. Ex: "What cause do you absolutely hate…? *Great. If you cancel early, I will be donating your setup fee to them.*" This gives them *two* reasons to stay. First, because they don't want to shell out the cash. Second, because they don't want a cause they hate to get it.

Exercise #22: Create Your Waived Fee Offer

Set up your two-option pricing model below.

- Monthly rate: $ _____
- Waived fee amount (*aim for 3–5x monthly rate*): $ _____
- Commitment length: _____ months

Now write out both offers:

Option A (Month-to-Month):

Pay $ _____ setup fee + $ _____ per month. *Cancel anytime.*

Option B (Commitment):

Waive the $ _____ setup fee if you commit to _____ months.

Pay $ _____ per month. Cancel early? Then pay the $ _____ fee.

FREE GIFT: Waive Fee Video Training

Waived fees are so so so effective. I can't wait for you to actually use them and see for yourself. To make sure you feel confident doing them on your own, I made you a video walking you through them. As usual, you can watch it free at acquisition.com/training/money. Or, you can scan the QR code. Enjoy.

Continuity Offers Conclusion

The only thing better than getting someone to buy once, is getting them to buy again.

Continuity Offers *provide ongoing value that customers make ongoing payments for until they cancel.* Many businesses use continuity offers to attract customers for less. But, it crashes 30-day profits. This makes profitable advertising difficult.

I use Continuity Offers differently. I make them *last.* I start with profitable Attraction Offers. Then make my Upsell and Downsell Offers. *Then,* I offer Continuity. And if they accept, I upsell a bulk amount of time or product at a discount. Then, they automatically enter continuity after they've used up their bulk purchase. This way, I make even more cash *and* I get the recurring-cash benefits of the other continuity customers.

Continuity Offers work with rewards or punishment. I prefer rewards. And two of the three Continuity Offers I explained use them. But, there will always be times when a more traditional contract makes sense. In those situations, I like Waived Fee Offers.

In the next section, we will create our $100M Money Model by combining all four offer types: Attraction Offers, Upsell Offers, Downsell Offers, and Continuity Offers.

Exercise #23: Pick Your Continuity Offer

Pick which continuity offers you will apply to your business:

    a. Continuity Bonus

    b. Continuity Discount

    c. Waived Fee Offer

SECTION VI: MAKE YOUR MONEY MODEL

How To Take Over Your Entire Market

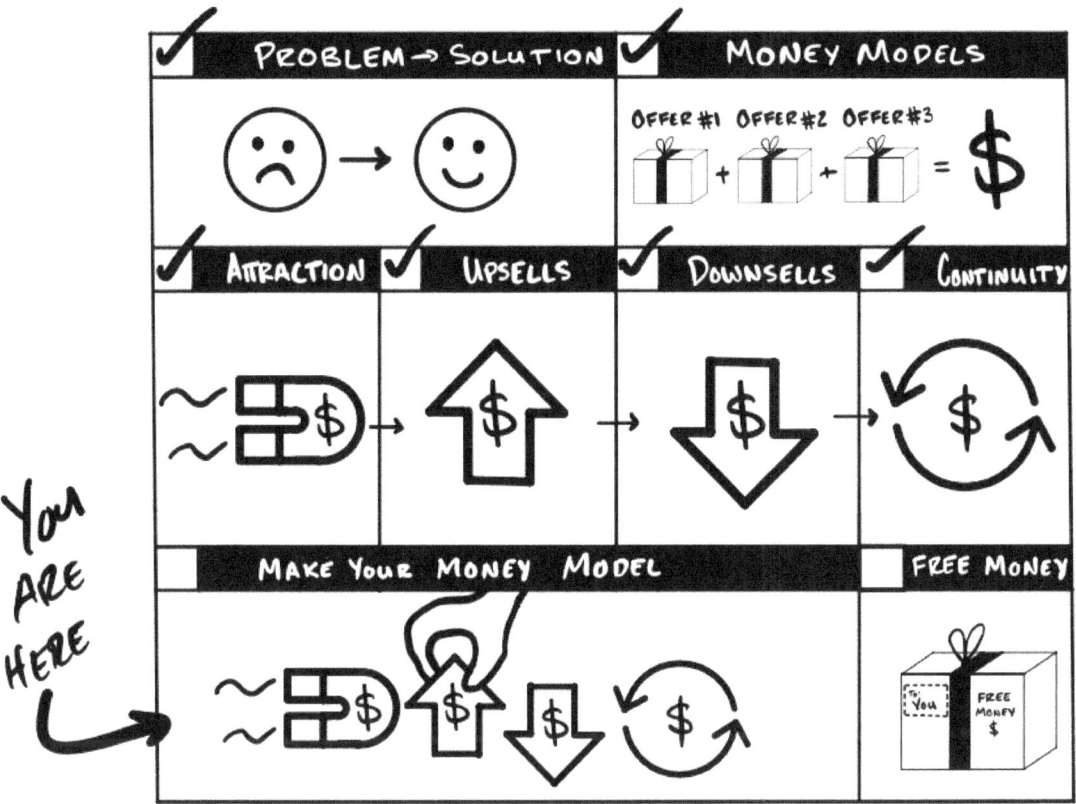

Looking back at the evolution of Gym Launch's $100M Money Model today.

My Gym Launch Model used many of the offers in this book to create a full-fledged $100M Money model.

- It all started with a Decoy Offer. I attracted new customers with lots of free courses, books, video training, live training, and so on. All stuff on growing a gym. Each free product came with its own free call to help gym owners use it. On the call I'd offer:

  - *Decoy Offer:* Now that you've got the plan, you do it on your own for free.

Or…

  - *Premium Offer:* We can help you implement all this stuff for $16,000 over 16 weeks. If they took the premium option, they'd get a treasure trove of money making tactics. Tactics that took me years to figure out. People bought left and right.

And whoosh, my Decoy Offer took me to $476,000 per month in three months. Not a typo.

- Then, I used the Classic Upsell to offer advanced playbooks, and services for $42,000 per year.

- And a Continuity Bonus of a community to share best practices.

- I started by offering a hefty *$6,000 discount* for anyone who prepaid.

- For the ones who didn't, I offered a Payment Plan Downsell.

- If they said no, I went for $10,000 down and spread the rest over time. If they said no again, I'd use a Continuity Discount to frontload the free time for as long as it took them to finish paying off the first offer. Then, they'd roll right into my continuity upsell. This way, their payments stayed continuous.

And zoom… The Classic Upsell + Continuity Bonus + Payment Plan Downsell + Continuity Discount took me to ~$1,500,000 per month.

- Even though the upsell and downsell process worked well, *some Gym Owners kept saying no*. I came up with a more personalized Menu Upsell with different levels of service.

- If they didn't want the whole package, I used Feature Downsells to find the best option for them. Almost everyone stayed for something.

And wham… Menu Upsells + Feature Downsells took me to $2,300,000 per month. All within 14 months.

- Then we started Prestige Labs and integrated it with Gym Launch. A totally different business with its own Money Model. By month 20, we were raking in $4,400,000 *per month*. It was life-changing. And it *only* took a *few darn good products* and a *$100M Money Model* to do it.

***

Description

A Money Model is *a deliberate sequence of offers*. It's what you offer, when you offer, and how you offer it to make as much money as you can as fast as you can. Ideally, to make enough money from one customer to get and service *at least* two more customers *in fewer than 30 days*. And it rarely looks clean, but I break $100M Money Models into three stages:

Stage I: Get Cash - Attraction Offers get more customers for less

Stage II: Get More Cash - Upsell & Downsell Offers make more money from them faster

Stage III: Get The Most Cash - Continuity Offers maximize their total money spent

In my experience, Money Models evolve like this:
- First, I get customers reliably *then*
- I make sure they pay for themselves reliably *then*
- I make sure they pay for other customers reliably *then*
- I start maximizing each customer's long-term value *then*
- I spend as many advertising dollars as I can to print as much money as possible.

My Money Models develop this way because I make sure *each stage pays for the next*. We keep improving each stage until it gets *reliable*. Also, this means financial *and* operational reliability.

Gym Launch's Money Models

Stage I Attraction Offer: Decoy Offer

Free Do-It-Yourself Decoy vs. Premium $16,000 Done-With-You licensing

Stage II Upsell Offer: Classic Upsell

Once you know how to get 'em, you gotta know how to keep 'em.

$42,000 per year ($36,000 prepaid) for advanced business services.

Stage II Downsell Offer: Payment Plan Downsell

Seesaw Downsell: *Start at $10,000 down with the rest spread over 52 weeks.*

Final Payment Plan Offer: *$800 per week for 52 weeks.*

Stage III Continuity Offer: Menu Upsell + Feature Downsell

Full Package: $800 per week

Feature—Done-For-You Advertising: $300 per week

Feature—Gym Sales Daily Training: $200 per week

Feature—Monthly New Releases: $500 per week

Feature—Original Licensing Materials with tech support: $100 per week

Minimum Package: $100 per week

<u>*If you want other examples, you can find them in the main book.*</u>

Make Your Own Money Model

Step 1) Start With An Attraction Offer. The goal is to turn strangers into customers and cover our costs. So, figure out what you're going to sell. Then, figure out the best way to present it. Pick from the five Attraction Offers, then, *advertise it*. If you get leads who turn into customers, you're on your way. Figuring out what works best may take up to a year. If you want to learn more about advertising, make sure to check out my second book *$100M Leads*.

Step 2) Pick An Upsell Offer. The goal is to get 30-day profits *well above* our costs of getting a new customer and delivering what you offer to them. Remember, once you solve a problem, another appears. Those problems also need solutions. You solve the problems your Attraction Offer creates with Upsell Offers. So pick the Upsell Offer that best matches the problem you solve and how you solve it. Then, make your offer at their time of greatest need.

Step 3) Pick A Downsell Offer. The goal is to get customers who said no to your last offer to say yes to another offer. This way, you'll sell *way more people* than you otherwise would—so you make more total cash *from the same number of leads*. The Downsell Offer section shows you my three favorites.

Step 4) Pick A Continuity Offer. The goal here is to get one last sale in our thirty-day window and stack recurring cash. So, I try to include continuity in business *eventually*.

Sometimes the best timing for continuity offers happens *after* the first 30 days, and that's OK. *It's better to make the offer at the right time than to try and force it at the wrong time.*

Important Notes

Perfect One Offer At A Time. It's tempting to implement a whole Money Model at once. Don't. Stick to your stage. Pick one offer. Try it. Keep doing it until it works reliably. Then, after it's reliable, do it so many times it gets automatic. *Then*, go to the next stage.

Raise Price In Stages. Make new offers cheap at first. Then, as you get yeses, raise the price. Lots of early yeses get customer feedback and make the product better. Then, as the offer gets reliable, start raising the price. And keep raising the price until the extra cash from the yeses doesn't make up for the nos.

Simple Scales. Fancy Fails. Get as much as you can out of what you have. Remember, it's less about having 100 products to offer, and more about having 100 ways to offer your product. Think more ways to sell the same thing, not more things to sell. *This turns one product into many offers.*

Turn Attraction Offers Into Continuity Offers With Automatic Renewal. This makes it a two-for-one. For example, if you do a Buy 6 Months Get 6 Months Free Offer, they can roll automatically into a month-to-month subscription at the end of 12 months. This gets the benefits of Attraction and Continuity Offers. A small tip with *big* implications.

You Can Mix And Match Offers However You Want. I present offers this way because that's how I use them. But if you recall, I learned many of them from people who used them differently than me! Many of these offers you can use *anywhere*. You can use Upsell tactics in your Attraction Offer. You can install a Downsell process with *every* offer. You can use a Continuity Offer to attract new customers. There are no rules. You can do whatever you want. I show you stuff one way, *but I fully expect you to use it in another.* So, start with the way I suggest it. Then, as you get better, experiment. It's how I learned this stuff. And it's how you'll learn it too.

Exercise #24: Assemble Your $100m Money Model

1. Pick your Attraction Offer: _____

2. Pick your Upsell Offer: _____

3. Pick your Downsell Offer(s): _____

4. Pick your Continuity Offer: _____

5. You now have the <u>final</u> version of your money model. It may take months (sometimes years) to fully build this out. That's okay. But now you know what you're building towards.

Exercise #25: List three different ways to sell the same thing:

Write your product below, then brainstorm three different ways to package, price, or offer it using the Money Model concepts.

My Product: _____

Offer Style	Description
Attraction Offer	_____
Upsell Version	_____
Continuity Version	_____

FREE GIFT: Make Your Own Money Model Step-By-Step Training

Whew. There's a lot in this chapter. It's also, arguably, the most important one in the book. So, to make sure you don't get stuck, I made you a video walking through this process step by step. As usual, you can watch it free (no opt-in needed) at acquisition.com/training/money. Or, you can scan the QR code.

Ten Years In Ten Minutes

The best thing a human can do is to help another human being know more. - Charlie Munger

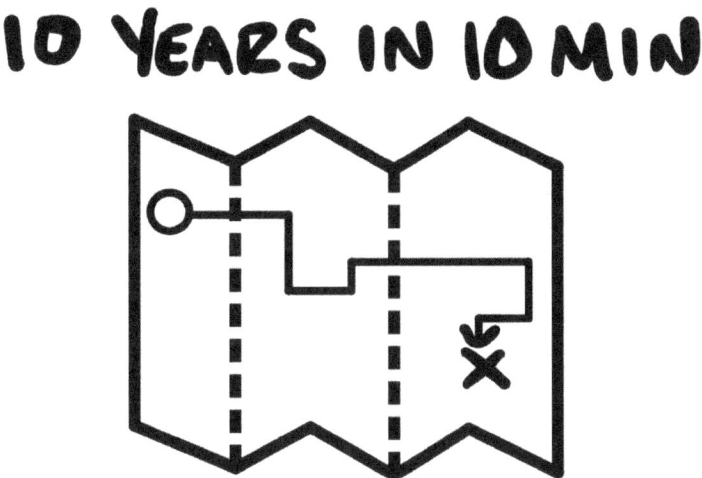

Where Money Models Fit In The Grand Scheme Of Things

- My first book, *$100M Offers*, answered the question: *What should I sell?* Answer: an offer so good people feel stupid saying no.

- My second book, *$100M Leads*, answered the next natural question: *How do I find these people?* Answer: You advertise.

- My third book, *$100M Money Models*, answers the next natural question: *How do I get them to buy it?* Answer: A Money Model.

- And hopefully, this workbook helped you do it.

What We Covered

We've covered a lot. And I think organizing what we learned into one place helps it sink in. So I made this "back of the napkin" list of what we've covered and why.

1) **A Money Model** is a series of offers designed to increase how many customers you get, how much they pay, and how fast they pay it.

2) **A good Money Model** *makes more profit from a customer than it costs to get and service them in the first 30 days.* That's the bare minimum.

3) **A $100M Money Model** *makes more profit from one customer than it costs to get and service many customers in the first 30 days,* which removes cash as a limiter to scaling your business.

4) Money Models have **four types of offers**: Attraction Offers, Upsell Offers, Downsell Offers, and Continuity Offers.

5) **Attraction Offers** get customers by offering something free or at a discount. Often, they also make money by offering a *better deal* at a higher price. We covered five.

   a) Win Your Money Back: *You* set a goal for the customer *and* tell them how to reach it. If they reach it, then they qualify to get their money back *or* get it back as store credit.

   b) Giveaways: You advertise a chance to win a big prize in exchange for contact information and anything else you want. After picking a winner, you offer everyone else the big prize at a discounted price.

   c) Decoy Offers: You advertise a free or discounted offer. When the lead asks to learn more, you *also* present a more valuable premium offer. The premium offer includes more features, benefits, bonuses, guarantees, and so on.

   d) Buy X Get Y Free: You offer customers free stuff in exchange for buying other stuff for money. The more free stuff and the higher its value, the more people buy.

   e) Pay Less Now or Pay More Later: You give people a choice to pay full price later OR pay a discounted price now *and* get additional bonuses.

6) **Upsell Offers** are whatever you offer next. Typically, more, better, or newer versions of what they just bought. These get you more cash fast. We covered four.

   a) The Classic Upsell: You offer the solution to the customer's next problem the moment they become aware of it. *You can't have X without Y!*

   b) Menu Upsells: You tell customers which options they don't need. Then, tell them what they do need *and* how to get their value from it. *You don't need that… you need this.*

   c) Anchor Upsells: You offer your most expensive thing first. If the customer balks, you offer a much-cheaper-and-still-acceptable-alternative. *No worries. If you don't care about X, this may be a better fit for you.*

d) Rollover Upsells: You credit some or all of a customer's previous purchases toward your next offer. *Since you already spent $500, I'll just credit that towards you staying a full year.*

7) **Downsell Offers** are whatever you offer after someone says no. And by turning Nos into Yeses you make more money. We covered three.

   a) Payment Plan Downsells: You offer the same product at the same price, but they pay some now and the rest over time. *When do you get paid? Let's do half now and half then?*

   b) Trial With Penalty: You let customers try your product or service for free *so long as they meet your terms.* If they do, they have a better chance of becoming paying customers. If they don't, they pay. *If you do X, Y, Z, I'll let you start for free.*

   c) Feature Downsells: You lower prices by changing what the customer gets. I offer lower quantity, lower quality, lower price alternatives, or cut optional components entirely. *If you're okay without a guarantee, I can knock off $400.*

8) **Continuity Offers** provide ongoing value that customers make ongoing payments for—until they cancel. These boost the profit of every customer and give you one last thing to sell. We covered three.

   a) Continuity Bonus Offers: You give the customer an awesome thing *if* they sign up today. Typically, the bonus itself has more value than the first continuity payment. *If you sign up today, you also get XYZ valuable thing.*

   b) Continuity Discounts Offers: You give the customer free time, now or later, *if* they sign up today.

   c) Waived Fee Offers: First, you ask the customer to pay a startup fee as part of joining a month-to-month program. Then, you offer to discount the *entire* fee *if* they commit longer term. If they cancel inside the term, they pay the fee.

9) You build Money Models **one stage at a time**.

   a) Once I get customers reliably *then* I make sure they pay for themselves reliably *then* I make sure they pay for other customers reliably *then* I start maximizing each customer's long term value. *Then*, I print as much money as I can.

Bottom line: The knowledge in these bullets brought me more free *and* profitable customers than I've known what to do with. If executed, they will do the same for you. And with that, cash will no longer constrain your business. I hope this book helps you grow your dream *as big as you darn well please.*

Also, since you are one of the few who actually finish what you start (even though this is shortened from the original), I want to leave you with a parting gift: some closing remarks that got me through hard times.

Final Thoughts

You don't become confident by shouting affirmations in the mirror.
You become confident by giving yourself a stack of undeniable proof
that you are who you say you are. Outwork your self-doubt.

An actual post I made on July 25, 2020. Before I made my life public.

***

Leila snapped this when I wasn't looking and I was like "DAYUMM I look pensive AF" 😄

Anyways, this is the second time we've taken a private jet.

And... it was dope.

They figure if you go down with the ship, your seatbelt won't save you.

Regardless - to every hard motherf*cker who is disappointing their parents, wives, husbands, friends, fake friends, and everyone else who doubts you.

#1 I AM YOUR BIGGEST FAN

#2 It's about to get real, so get hard fast

#3 You cannot lose if you do not quit. I used to repeat that to myself over and over when I didn't want to keep doing it. If you feel hopeless... welcome to entrepreneurship. If you feel like you'll never make it... you're on the right path. If you feel like you're a disappointment to everyone you know... keep f*cking moving.

Because at the end of the rainbow isn't a pot of gold.

It's you.

The real you.

That's been underneath all along whispering in your ear—just one more step.... one more call... one more sale.

When I say I'm your biggest fan, it's because I was there. And I know you because I know EXACTLY what that FEELS like. Having both 100% confidence and 1,000% doubt. At the same time. Here's all you gotta do:

Just keep moving.

Keep fighting.

Keep improving.

Your time will come.

Success is the only revenge.

***

So right now you might be where I was back when I started. Working in a concrete coffin, under blinding fluorescent lights, wanting to escape. You might be overwhelmed by all the stuff you have to do to succeed. But with that uncertainty, know that every entrepreneur, past and present, shoulders the burden with you. I've been there. They've been there. You are not alone. I share these stories as I experienced them so you can benefit from them as I have.

So here's my promise: follow the lessons, the money will come.

Be one of zero.

Alex Hormozi, Founder, Acquisition.com

PS - I've got some free goodies for you for finishing what you started.

Free Goodies

Nom nom nom.

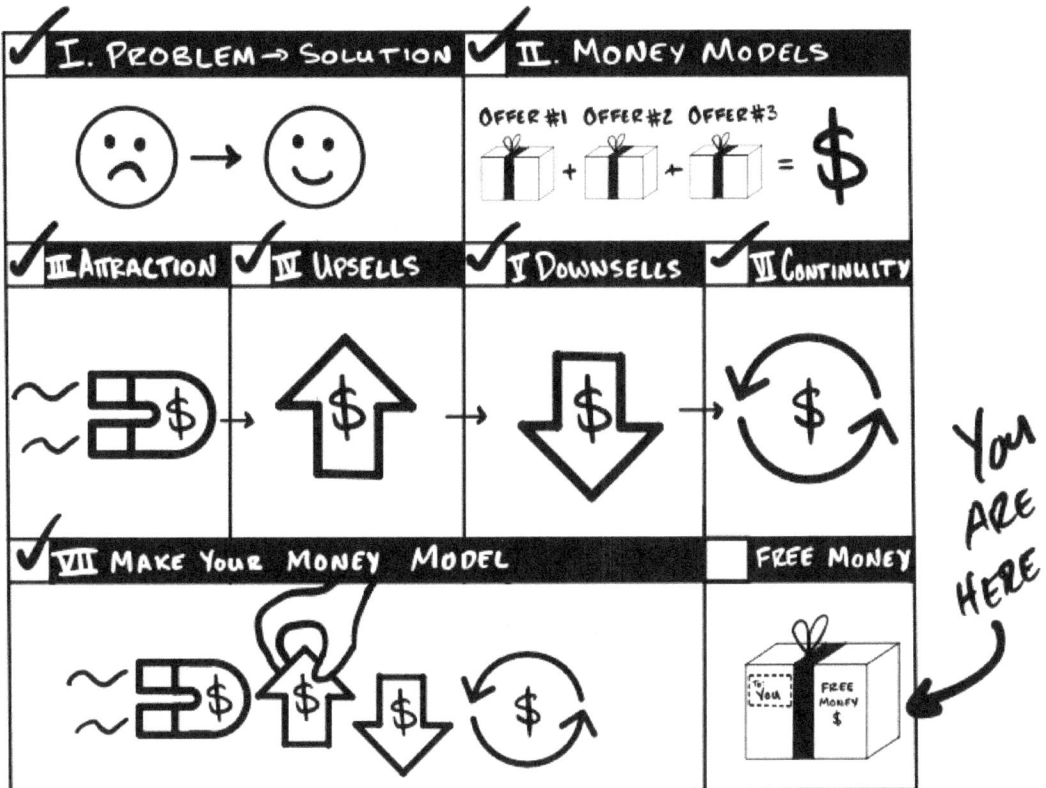

Kinda like the previews after the credits finish, if you're still with me, I wanted to give you a bunch of goodies.

1) **If you're struggling to figure out who to sell to**, I released a chapter called "Your First Avatar." You can get it for free at **Acquisition.com/avatar.** Just pop in your email and we'll send it over.

2) **If you're struggling to figure out what to sell**, you can go to Amazon or wherever you buy books and search "Alex Hormozi" and *$100M Offers*. It should get you on the right path.

3) **If you're struggling to get people interested in what you sell,** you can go to Amazon or wherever you buy books and search "Alex Hormozi" and *$100M Leads*. It should get you on the right path.

4) **If your company is over $1M in EBITDA (profit)**, we'd love to help you scale. It brings so much pleasure to know companies have grown much bigger and faster than mine *because they avoided the mistakes I made*. If you want us to take a look under the hood and see if we can help go to **Acquisition.com**.

5) **If you want a job at Acquisition.com** or in one of our companies—we love hiring from #mozination. Our best returns come from investing in great people. Go to **Acquisition.com/careers/open-jobs**, and you can see all the available openings.

6) To get the **free book downloads and video trainings** that come with this book, go to **Acquisition.com/training/money**.

7) **If you like listening to podcasts and want to hear more**, my podcast at the time of this writing is top five in entrepreneurship and top 15 in business in the US. You can get there by searching "Alex Hormozi" wherever you listen. Or, by going to **Acquisition.com/podcast**. I share useful and interesting stories, valuable lessons, and the essential mental models I rely on every day.

8) **If you like to watch videos**, we put a lot of resources into our free training, available for everyone. We intend on making it better than any paid stuff out there, and let you decide if we succeeded. You can find our videos on YouTube or wherever you watch videos by searching "Alex Hormozi."

9) **And if you like short-form videos**, check out the bite-sized content we pump out daily at **Acquisition.com/media**. You'll see all the places we post and you can pick the ones you like the most.

And last, thank you again. Please be one of those givers and **share this with other entrepreneurs by leaving a review**. It would mean the world to me. I'm sending you business building vibes from my desk. I spend a lot of time there, so it's a lot of vibes. May your desire be greater than your obstacles.

www.ingramcontent.com/pod-product-compliance
Lightning Source LLC
Chambersburg PA
CBHW082023050526
44107CB00101B/635